The Atmosphere of Cornwall

An evocative view of Cornwall photographed by BOB CROXFORD

There is something wonderful, I think, about the land of Cornwall. That long peninsula extending out into the ocean has caught all sorts of strange floating things, and has held them there in isolation until they have woven themselves into the texture of the Cornish race.

Arthur Conan Doyle from Through the Magic Door   1907

Published by ATMOSPHERE

In memory of Becky who I miss so much

The Atmosphere of Cornwall

ISBN 978 0 9550805 2 4

Photography Copyright Bob Croxford 2008
Original Text Copyright Bob Croxford 2008
Design Copyright Ann Butcher and Atmosphere

Anthology compiled by Karen Forster & Bob Croxford

First Published by ATMOSPHERE in 2008

Willis Vean

Mullion

Helston Cornwall TR12 7DF

Tel: 01326 240180

Fax: 01326 240900

All rights reserved. No part of this book may be reproduced by any means without prior consent from the copyright holders.

Designed by Ann Butcher
Printed and bound in Italy by Esaprint

Frontispiece: Pednevounder Beach

Also by BOB CROXFORD

FROM CORNWALL WITH LOVE	978 0 9521850 0 0
FROM DEVON WITH LOVE	0 9521850 1 6
FROM BATH WITH LOVE	0 9521850 2 4
FROM THE COTSWOLDS WITH LOVE	978 0 9521850 4 8
FROM DORSET WITH LOVE	978 0 9521850 3 1
A VIEW OF AVALON	0 9521850 6 7
THE CORNISH COAST	0 9521850 7 5
CORNISH RECIPES	978-0-9543409-9-5
ST IVES	978-0-9550805-1-7
CORNWALL FROM THE AIR	978 0 9543409 4 0
NORTH DEVON	0 9521850 8 3
THE SOUTH HAMS	0 9521850 9 1
THE DORSET COAST	978-0-9543409-0-2
AVEBURY	0 9543409 1 4
THE COTSWOLDS	0 9543409 2 2
SOUTH DEVON - THE ENGLISH RIVIERA	0 9543409 3 0
DARTMOOR	0 9543409 5 7
EXETER AND THE EXE	0 9543409 6 5
HAMPSHIRE	0 9543409 7 3
BATH	0 9543409 8 1
PLYMOUTH	978-0-9550805-3-1
PORTSMOUTH	978-0-9550805-4-8

INTRODUCTION	8-9
FROM THE TAMAR TO THE FOWEY	10-20
FROM THE FOWEY TO THE HELFORD	21-31
FROM THE HELFORD TO PORTHLEVEN	32-41
FROM ST MICHAEL'S MOUNT TO SENNEN	42-51
FROM GURNARD'S HEAD TO WATERGATE BAY	52-63
FROM PORTHCOTHAN TO BUDE	64-77
INLAND	78-85
INDEX AND CAPTIONS	86-89
LIST OF WRITERS	89
MAP	91
PHOTOGRAPHER'S NOTES	92
ACKNOWLEDGEMENTS	93

Cornwall has an ambiance like no other county. With cliffs, beaches, coves and estuaries its coastline is rich and varied. The climate will vary from summers of heat wave and drought to those of almost continuous rain. The winters are often mild but can also have severe gales and occasional blizzards. In the time that the megalithic stone circles, quoits and standing stones were built Cornwall was one of the most densely populated parts of Britain. Man's impact on the landscape has lasted several thousand years. The landscape has also impacted on the inhabitants making them a uniquely resourceful people.

Fifteen years ago I produced a book of my photographs called 'From Cornwall With Love'. It was a shot in the dark and a big risk for me. I worried long and hard about such a big investment on one project. I need not have been so anxious. So successful was it that the first edition sold out in three months. Now fifteen years, and many reprints later, I have decided to do a second volume. Like the first it is a collection of evocative images which together form a portrait of the beauty of Cornwall. As a counterpoint to the images the book also includes an anthology of writing on Cornwall, past and present.

Much has changed since 1993 and the photography I did then. As the world has become less optimistic my photography has become a bit more hard edged. While the subjects remain beautiful my view of them has become more straightforward, sharper and tighter.

In the first book's introduction I deplored some of the changes which were taking place in Cornwall. In the intervening years the pace has accelerated. The number of supermarkets has increased while the number of village shops and post offices has dropped. Some of the post offices who supported me by stocking my books have now closed. Cornwall is the poorest county in the country and despite slowly improving prosperity the rest of the country is becoming richer quicker. The gap between local wages and house prices is the greatest in Britain.

The population has increased more than almost any other area of Britain. Cornwall is now considered the most desirable destination to live in the country. Young people have moved away to find jobs and ever greater numbers of people move to Cornwall until towns, villages, schools and hospitals nearly burst at the seams. Mining has stopped altogether despite a handful of brave attempts to revive it. Farming has changed as milk prices fall and costs rise. Where cows once grazed now thousands of foreign workers replace locals in the fields. Fishing too, has declined under a flood of government regulation.

Thankfully the coastline hasn't changed too much. Cornwall still boasts some of the most beautiful scenery in the world. Despite the activities of developers intent on building some of the ugliest buildings imaginable many of our villages and towns still retain some aspects of a distinctive character.

The anthology of Cornish writing in the first book included research culled from A L Rowse's 'Cornish Anthology' and Ian Martin's 'Literary Trails'. At the time I thought it might be impossible to repeat the idea with another set of quotations. So much has been written about Cornwall over the years that it was easier than I thought. The poetic praise, the ironic remarks, the historic observations, the downright insults and the unbridled compliments added together make a potpourri of opinion. Reading some of the historic writings shows that little has changed. Lack of prosperity led to great ingenuity in the past just as it does in the present. Jokes at the expense of 'foreigners' or 'emmets' are remarkably similar, whether told 200 years ago or in the present day.

Cornwall has now established itself as a popular setting for books, films and TV dramas. Following the earlier 'Poldark' series there is 'Doc Martin' set in the fictional village of 'Portwenn', where Martin Clunes seems to get mobile phone reception everywhere unlike the real village of Port Isaac where it was filmed. Portloe stood in for 'St Gweep' in the series 'Wild West'. Probably the most famous TV series are the ones made by German TV of the Rosamunde Pilcher novels. Screened at peak time in Germany and Austria many Germans now refer to Cornwall as 'Rosamund Pilcher Country'. Films have brought Dame Judi Dench and Maggie Smith to Prussia Cove for Charles Dance's 'Ladies in Lavender' and James Bond to Holywell Bay standing in for North Korea in 'Goldeneye' which also featured the Eden Project Biomes.

National journalists pay for their summer breaks by running off a few hundred words on the glories of Cornwall. The county has almost become a celebrity where even the cooks, sorry, Michelin starred chefs, get national recognition.

The success of my first and subsequent books has been due to the many small shopkeepers who stocked and helped promote it over the years. Sadly, many have closed and with post office closures many small shops will find it harder to survive in the future. Hopefully the ingenuity which has served Cornwall well over the years will help the county survive into the future.

Bob Croxford   2008

One hundred years ago the orchards of the Tamar valley were prolific; the whole area was famous for its extraordinary variety of fruit and the springtime blossom. 'A lot of fruit,...was sent by river to Devonport market but once the railway arrived at Plymouth in 1849, London and the Midlands became a big market - Tamar cherries sold all over the country at 2d and 5d a pound.

Derek Cooper from
Snail Eggs and Samphire 2000

Dawn rain cleared as we entered Cornwall under augury of dissolving rainbows, giving the little round hills an added remoteness, with their few square cottages, clumps of bush and stunted tree, grey stone hedges: an increased greenness: a shutness. This contributed far more excitement to the strangeness of first light - of silvery and slightly golden light - as the train charged through it, than crossing the tall suicidal bridge over the Tamar of Brunel, which made everything seem so small. This in turn added to the feeling of metamorphosis taking place inside me as our discovery of the future began.

Sven Berlin from Pride of the Peacock   1972

‹ *Calstock Viaduct and River Tamar*
   Brunel's Royal Albert Bridge across the Tamar ›

The Cornish drolls are dead, each one;
The fairies from their haunts have gone:
There's scarce a witch in all the land,
The world has grown so learn'd and
grand.

Henry (Henna) Quick 1792-1857

St. Piran came over from Ireland in a coracle, and, like a prudent man, brought with him a bottle of whisky. On landing on the north coast he found that there was a hermit there named Chigwidden. The latter was quite agreeable to be friends with the new-comer, who was full of Irish tales, Irish blarney, and had, to boot, a bottle of Irish whisky. Who would not love a stranger under the circumstances? Brothers Chigwidden and Piran drank up the bottle.

"'By dad,' said Piran, 'bothered if there be another dhrop to be squeezed out! Never mind, my spiritual brother, I'll show you how to distil the crayture. Pile me up some stones, and we'll get up the devil of a fire, and we shall make enough to expel the deuce out of ould Cornwall.'

"So Chigwidden collected a number of black stones, and the two saints made a fine fire — when, lo! out of the black stones thus exposed to the heat ran a stream like liquid silver. Thus was tin discovered."

Henry C Shelley from   Untrodden English Ways 1908

‹ Cawsand
Kingsand ›

*F*rom here we look down on Looe, or rather on the two Looes, for there is a Looe on each side of the river, a cluster of closely-packed white houses clinging to the steep banks of a very narrow estuary. Everything is on a toy scale. It has toy beaches, a toy pier in the shape of a banjo, a toy harbour, and even the river, as it winds among the trees, seems to disappear into Lilliputian creeks. There are toy islands and toy rocks, and the seven-arched stone bridge connecting the two towns, in comparison with those at Bideford, Barnstaple, Saltash, and Calstock, seems a toy one.

S P B Mais from The Cornish Riviera 1928

‹ *A fishing boat leaves Looe*
Banjo Pier, Looe ›

We featherstitched off to Looe. It was very hot—all glowing and quiet with loud birds singing and the blue-bells smelled like honey. The approach to Looe is amazing, it's not English, certainly not French or German. I must wait to describe it. The hotel buggy met us driven by a white-haired very independent boy who drove the horse as though it were a terribly fierce ramping white dragon—just to impress us, you know. We drove through lanes like great flowery loops with the sea below and huge gulls sailing over or preening themselves upon the roof tiles, until we came to this hotel which stands in its garden facing the open sea. It could not be a more enchanting position. The hotel is large, "utterly first-class," dreadfully expensive.

Katherine Mansfield from
Letters May 17, 1918

I rode, through heavy rain to Polperro. Here the room over which we were to lodge being filled with pilchards and conger-eels, the perfume was too potent for me; I was not sorry when one of our friends invited me to lodge at her house.

From The Journal of JOHN WESLEY Friday 16 September 1768

On the one hand I see Cornwall impoverished by the evil days on which mining and (to a lesser degree) agriculture have fallen. I see her population diminishing and her able-bodied sons forced to emigrate by the thousand, the ruined engine-house, the roofless cottage, the cold hearthstone are not cheerful sights to one who would fain to see a race so passionately attached to home as ours is still drawing vigour from its soil. In the presence of destitution and actual famine (for in the mining district it came even to this, a little while ago) one is bound, if he cares for his countrymen, to consider any cure thoughtfully suggested.

The suggestion is that Cornwall should turn her natural beauty to account, and by making it more widely known, at once benefit thousands and honestly enrich herself.

Sir Arthur Quiller-Couch from the Cornish Magazine 1898

‹ A swan glides across Polperro's inner harbour
Polperro ›

The editor of this work, from his own observation, will venture to assert, that there is no county in England presenting greater opportunities of success in agricultural speculation, than Cornwall.

Topography of Great Britain 1805

S pring and autumn are the loveliest periods to be in Cornwall. Summer has its own marvels, of course, but in most recent years these have been almost swamped by a positive avalanche of holidaymakers, bringing with them an incredible assortment of appendages - cars, caravans, motor coaches, tents, trailers, boats. At least this means new faces and new personalities, an infusion of liveliness and independence that is good and salutary for a corner of England that tends to be isolationist. If only they did not have to bring all that weaponry with them! As soon as the schools break up all roads to Cornwall become jammed with long queues of new arrivals, hotels, boarding houses and most private houses are full to overflowing, while green fields everywhere - often in the most beautiful and tranquil beauty spots - sprout rashes of coloured tents.

Denys Val Baker from Spring at Land's End 1974

‹ *Pencarrow Head*
Lanteglos-by-Fowey ›

I think Fowey means more to me than anything now. The river, the harbour, the sea. It's much more than love for a person. I don't know how I am going to exist back in London,...

Daphne du Maurier from her Diary 1928

One of the pleasures of travelling this fractured coast was such a vista. The irregularity of the English coast offered unusually long views, and these heights helped. A vantage point like the Gribbin made this part of Cornwall look like a topographical map with raised features in bright colours - the best views were always like dazzling maps. And in contrast to the sea, there were the reassuring pastures: on one side the cows and bees and sheep, and slate walls and the smell of manure, and on the other side the gulls and cormorants and whiff of salt spray; and these mingled. The gulls crossed into the pastures, the crows strutted on the sand, and the smells of muck and salt mingled, too.

Paul Theroux from The Kingdom by the Sea 1984

A toy town to look at on a bay so small, hemmed in so picturesquely by cliffs and ruins that of a moonlit night it might pass for a scene in a theatre.

J M Barrie 1892

‹ *Boat at Polruan*
Fowey ›

Mevagissey was a pretty little fishing village, with houses and fish-cellars crowded together and streets so narrow that for most of their length only the smallest of wagons were able to pass each other.

There was an inner and outer harbour and both were crowded with boats. These were mainly fishing vessels; only half-a-dozen had steam engines. The remainder were sailing vessels, their owners reliant upon the vagaries of the wind to earn a living.

A smell of fish pervaded the whole village and was especially strong in the harbour area. Many boats had come in on a rising tide and their cargoes were being unloaded in large quantities by men in heavy boots and faded, baggy jerseys.

E V Thompson from The Lost Years 2002

In 1957, Cornwall was still something of a backwater. Even in Plymouth, there were still large areas of bomb-damaged houses, and not many new blocks of flats or shops. St. Austell and Mevagissey probably looked as they had in 1900 (when Bernard Shaw used to come down here on holiday). The pubs were shabby, dark and homely, with a tendency to be divided into several small bars and 'dens'. Post-war prosperity was slowly increasing the holiday traffic, but the Cornish had not given much thought to the question of how to exploit it. The quay in Mevagissey was still largely a matter of fish warehouses, with the occasional small shop. It was clear that there was money to be made with commercial acumen, but no one was quite sure how.

Colin Wilson from My Cornwall 1973

❮ *Red Floats*
Colourful boats in Mevagissey Harbour ❯

Corineus, however, following in this the example of his leader, called the region of the kingdom which had fallen to his share Cornwall, after the manner of his own name, and the people who lived there he called Cornishmen.

Geoffrey of Monmouth from Historia Regum Britanniæ c. 1136

Me yv duk in oll Kernow
indella ytho ov thays
hag vhel arluth in pov
a t amer the pen an vlays
tregys off lemen heb wov
berth in castel an dynas
sur in peddre
ha war an tyreth vhel
thym yma castel arel
a veth gelwys tyndagyel
henna vy o(v) fenn tregse

(I am the Duke of Cornwall:
So was my father,
And a high lord in the country
From Tamar to Land's End.
I am dwelling now, without a lie,
Within the castle of Dynas
Surely in Pidar,
And in the high land
I have another castle,
Which is called Tintagel:
That is my chief dwelling-seat.)

From Beunans Meriasek 15th century

‹ Charlestown Harbour
 King Harry Ferry ›

*T*ruro, with a population of about twelve thousand, has twelve policemen, while Helston, with a population of four thousand, has only one; and not only is this active individual a policeman, but he holds also a number of other offices - he is sanitary inspector, surveyor, inspector of weights and measures, and borough messenger.

From The West Briton 1879

They were in the forest of Moresk; That night they lay on the hill. Now Tristan is as safe as if he were in a castle with a wall.

Tell him that he knows the marsh well, at the end of the plank-bridge at Malpas: There, I soiled my clothes a little. On the mound, at the end of the plank-bridge, and a little this side of the Lande Blanche, let him be dressed in the clothes of a leper; let him carry a wooden cup, let him have a bottle beneath tied on with a strap; in the other hand, let him carry a stick. This is the stratagem he must keep in mind.

Beroul 12th century

‹ *The Tresillian River at Malpas*
Truro Cathedral ›

Indeed, along this Cornish coast, life and death seem very near together. Every pleasure carries with it a certain amount of risk; the utmost caution is required both on land and sea, and I cannot advise either rash or nervous people to go travelling in Cornwall.

An Unsentimental Journey Through Cornwall by Dinah Craik   1884

The Cornish are remarkable for their sanguine temperament, their indomitable perseverance, their ardent hope in adventure, and their desire for discovery and novelty; hence their wide distribution all over the world, in the most remote corners of which they are to be found amongst the pioneers; and to this very cause has science to boast of so many brilliant ornaments who claim Cornwall as their birthplace.

George Henwood   1859

‹ Old Kea Church
An old rowing boat at Combe ›

We parted the trees and looked out on the peaceful beauty of the creek; the tide coming up, the high, still woods, and beyond, the deep waters of Carrick Roads. 'Incredible, unspoilt beauty!'

H V Morton from
In Search of England 1964

F*almouth is a most noteworthy and celebrated harbour, and in one sense is the most important in the whole of Britain. For the channel in its mouth, usually known as Carrick Roads, extends two miles upstream, to a depth of fourteen fathoms, and so offers a safe refuge for even the largest of ocean-going ships.*

John Leland's Itinerary 16th century

‹ *Sailing boats at Falmouth*
Falmouth Docks and The National Maritime Museum ›

The Helford oysters were cooked correctly, were delicious and nourishing and how I liked to think of their river's romantic colour and verdant banks. It means more to my spirit than Fal or Camel. Seldom are rivers the hue of jade.

C C Vyvyan from A Cornish Year   1958

Helford River, Helford River, Blessed may ye be! We sailed up Helford River By Durgan from the sea.

Arthur Quiller-Couch 1863-1944

There certainly is no doubt that Helford harbour, the Little Dinas, and Condurra, were objects of attention to every enemy (to pirates often) from the Romans to the present time.... I cannot but express my wonder that the French should have left us so long unmolested; that not even a privateer should have approached us, in our present defenceless state; for not one gun have we on the Little Dinas, not one vessel in the harbour of Helford to guard us from the invader. In the late war, on my representation, a gun-vessel was sent to us without delay; and preparations were made for fortifying the Dinas."

Letter from Rev Richard Polwhele   1826

‹ Helford Estuary
Helford Creek ›

Helston, metropolis of Meneage, with its tilted cross of lights and the gurgle and lapse of water in the street runnels, dims behind us. We are heading towards the south, out by Culdrose along the last ribbon of Cornish road that spans the peninsula of the Lizard. At its end you must either return the same way or take a high dive in the foam........

J C Trewin from Up from the Lizard 1948

She took me to see her aunt's house, high up on the cliffs, towards the Lizard, the most southerly tip of Cornwall. She knew everybody, Henry and Rene Jane who lived up the hill, the other side of the village, welcomed us with open arms. Henry had great bushy eyebrows and Rene was a jolly motherly figure. We sat in her kitchen while she made pasties, real home-made pasties.

I went fishing with Henry and his friend Buller, crabbing with pots. Their boat was called Minerva. The fishing boats were launched down the beach in the early dawn on timbers and winched up when they came home on a winch installed in 1910. All the fishermen had nicknames; Lamby and Bunny, Jimma, Sharkey and Rambo. Nina called them 'The Beastly Fishermen'.

Rodney Bewes from his autobiography A Likely Story 2005

‹ Coverack harbour
　Cadgwith ›

I never saw anything like the wonderful colour of the serpentine rocks, rich, deep, warm, variegated, mottled and streaked and veined with red, green and white, huge blocks and masses of precious stone marble on every side, an enchanted cove, the palace of the Nereids.

Francis Kilvert at Kynance Cove in 1870

Yet how beautiful it all was! Many a night afterwards we watched the same scene, but never lovelier than that night, the curved line of coast traceable distinctly up to Mount's Bay, and then the long peninsula which they told us was the Land's End, stretching out into the horizon, where sea and sky met in a mist of golden light, through which the sun was slowly dropping night from the sky into the sea. Beyond was a vague cloud-land, which might be the fair land of Lyonesse itself, said still to lie there submerged, with all its cities and towers and forests; or the 'Island-valley of Avilion,' whither Arthur sailed with the three queens to be healed of his 'grievous wound,' and whence he is to come again some day. Popular superstition still expects him, and declares that he haunts this coast even now in the shape of a Cornish chough.

Dinah Craik from An Unsentimental Journey Through Cornwall   1884

‹ Coast path with sea pinks
Kynance Cove ›

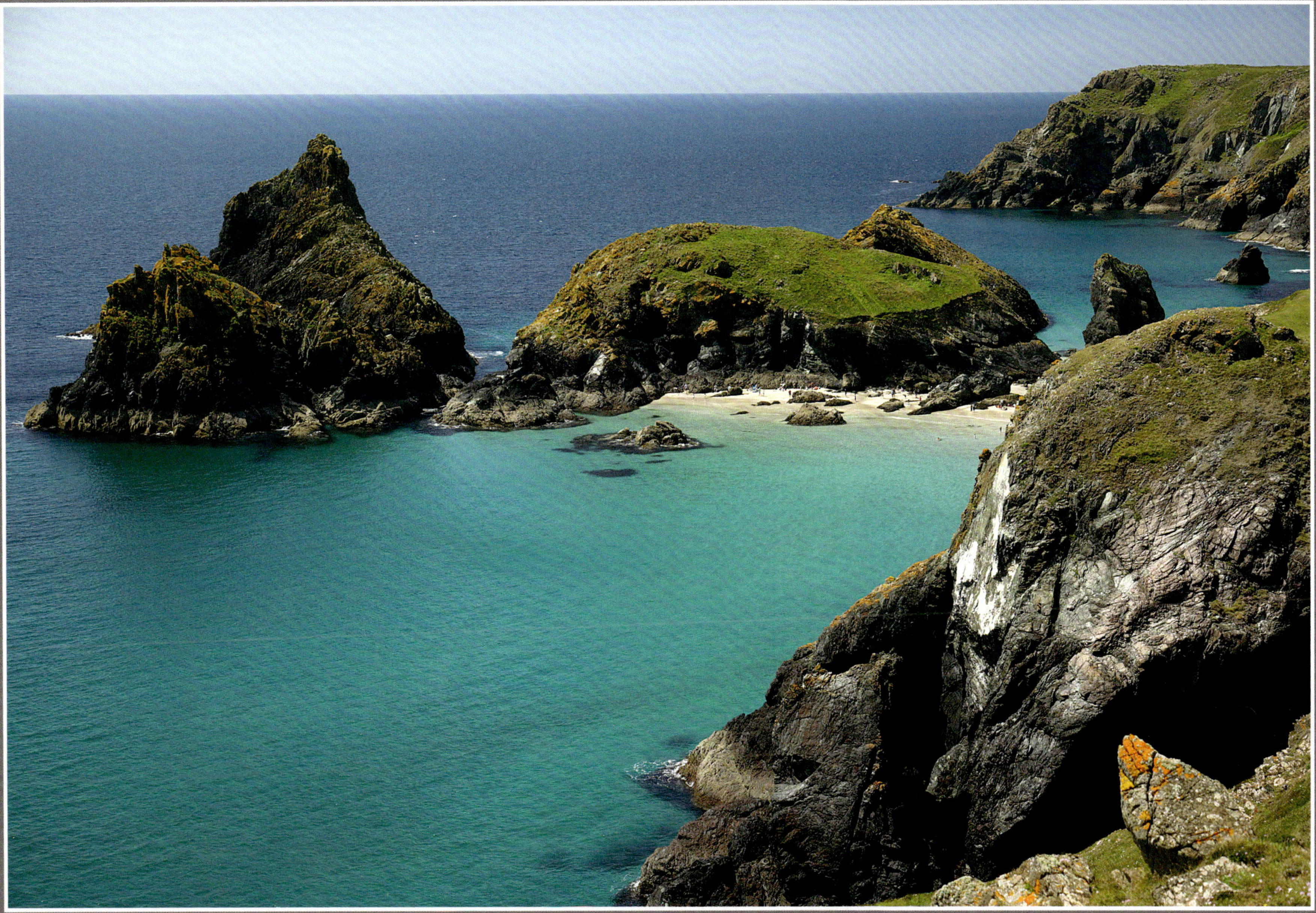

Gunwalloe Church Cove

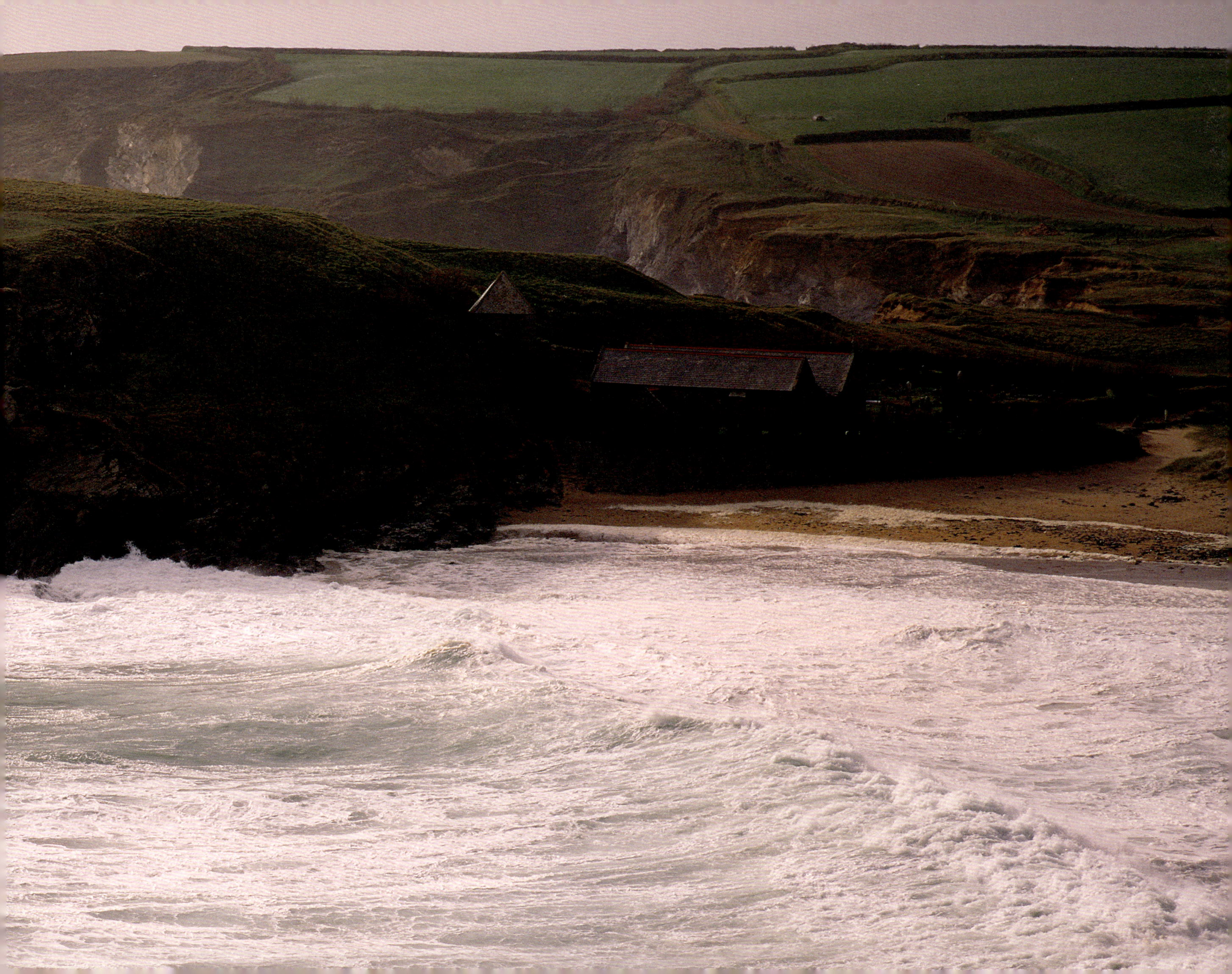

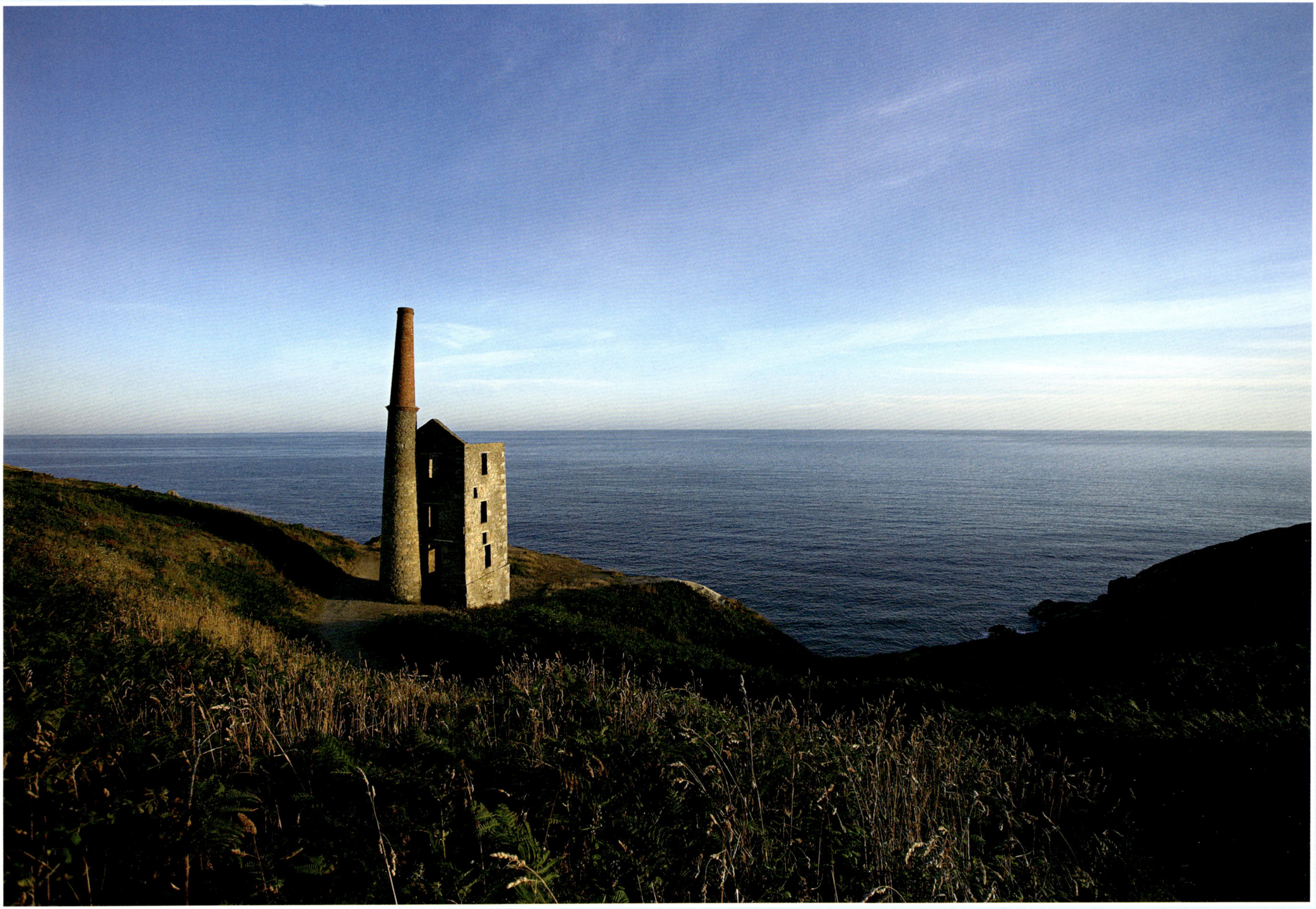

The location we found, near Penzance, had everything. Cottage, beach, cliffs, the lot. We could sit there for a large part of the shoot, thereby saving time and money. There would be logistical problems about getting people and equipment up and down from the cottage to the beach, but like all our other problems they would be solved - they would have to be."

Charles Dance from his Diary on the making of Ladies in Lavender   2004

It is said that more than 100 emigrants left Cornwall last week. The stream of emigrants, in fact, shows no ebb, but still runs on, as fast and deep as ever. Another 80 bid friends and relatives au revoir on Friday morning from the Western Division, being conveyed to Southampton by a special train chartered by the G.W.R., and personally dispatched by the Penzance officials. The western terminus on Friday morning was densely thronged by a large gathering, composed of emigrants and those who had assembled to wish them bon voyage, the latter being considerably in the majority. Luggage was, of course plentiful, and one immigrant took with him a typical greyhound, while another, evidently fond of feathered pets, had a bird and cage. Tears were, naturally, plentiful, and only those who say "good-bye" for perhaps the last time to a loving father, a dearly loved son and brother, or a near friend, know what it is.

From The West Briton   1898

❮ Wheal Prosper at Rinsey
   Porthleven Harbour ❯

This sublime spectacle is situate within the range of the parish of St Hilary, and is one of those rare and singular objects, which impress the mind with sensations of veneration, pleasure, and astonishment the instant it is seen : its situation is about thirteen miles from the most western land in England, in the inmost recess of the Mount's Bay. This mountain, which is surrounded with the sea six hours out of twelve, is about four hundred yards from the shores of Marazion. At its base it is upwards of a mile in circumference; and from the sand which lies around it, to the summit of the tower crowning its apex, is about two hundred and fifty feet. At high water it appears, from its being insulated, and from that vast expanse of horizon which is seen in every direction, to be considerably diminished in its circumference; but even this variation adds much to the beauty and enchantment of the scene; ...

John Thomas from Ancient and Modern History of Mount's Bay   1831

There is no part of England that abounds so much in the necessaries and at the same time has so many of the elegancies of life as that of Mount's Bay. The gentry, most of whom are our near relations, are of a free frolicking disposition. In the summer time we meet (some ten or a dozen) at a bowling green; there we have built a little pleasure-house and there we dine...

Letter from William Borlase b 1696

‹ St Michael's Mount
The causeway at St Michael's Mount ›

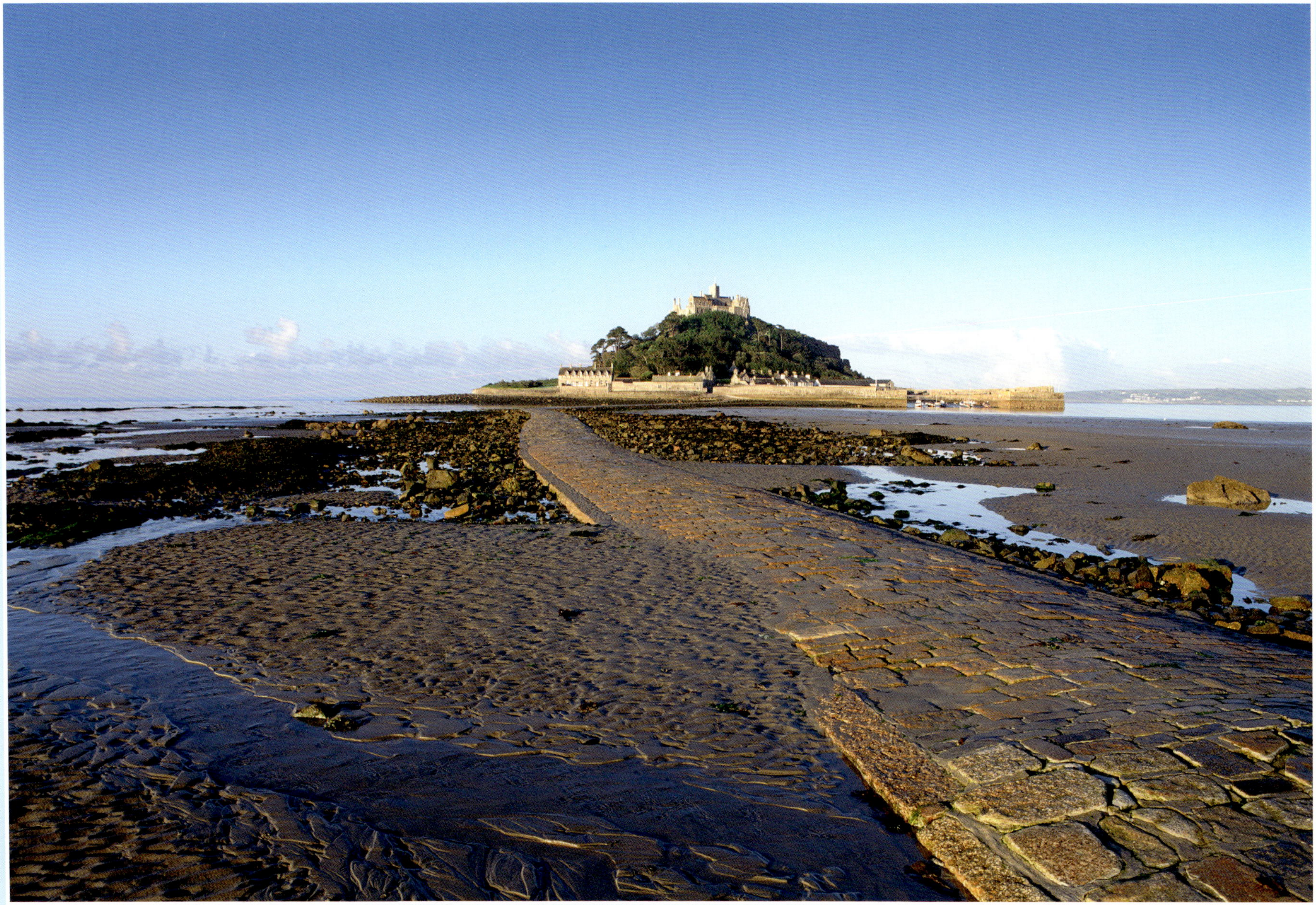

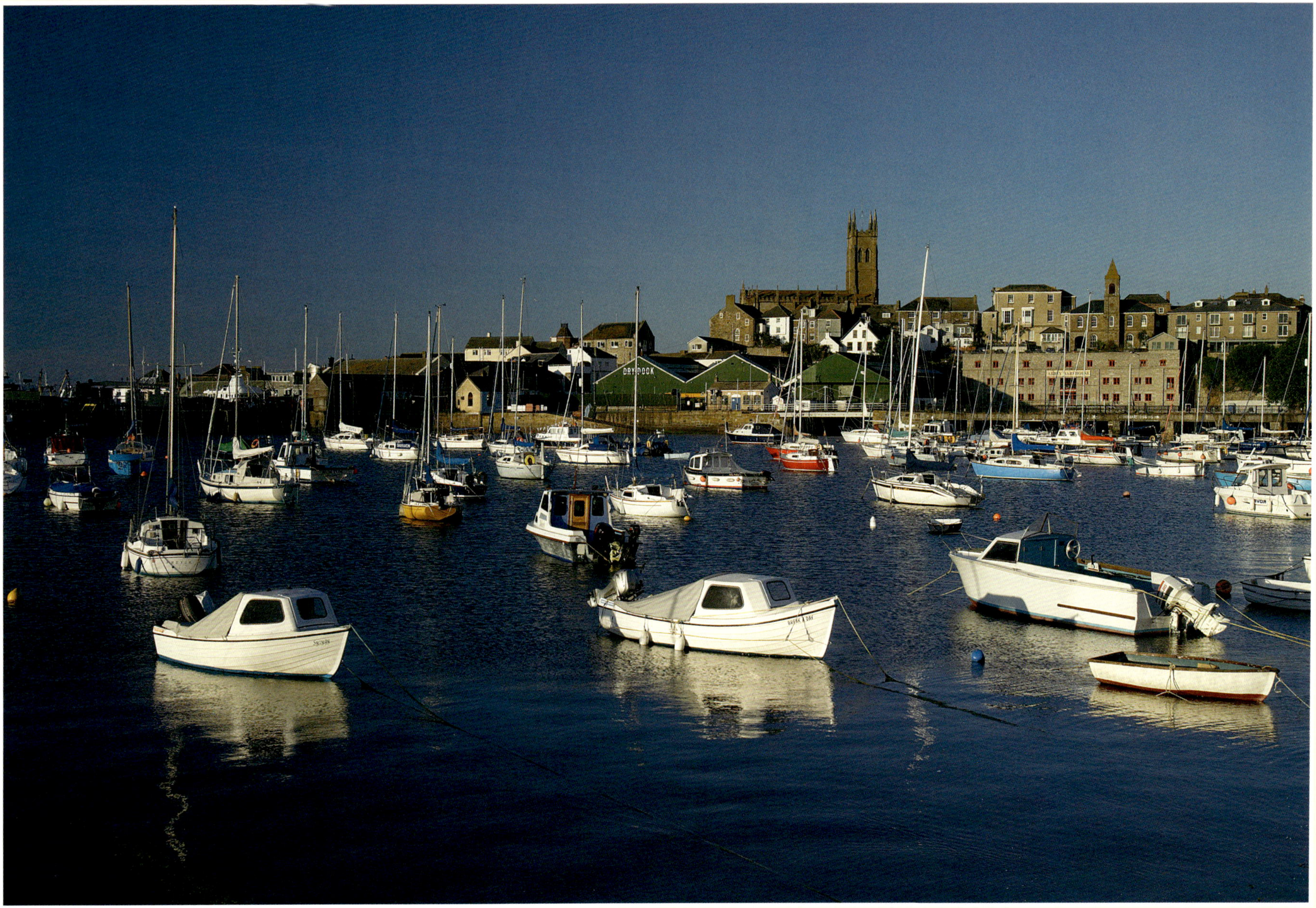
DRY DOCK

Thomas Mills, the Bristol journalist (who) toured West Cornwall in 1863. He, with a friend, had walked from Penzance to Lamorna, and being thirsty, had been directed to a "tiddly-wink." He wrote, "Well, I must say I like Cornwall, I like Cornish men and women, and fish and scenery, but I don't like Cornish beer....such beer as you meet with in out-of-the-way places, like that at La Morna. I understand it is not made from malt or hops, but from a fermented preparation of treacle and water...it can be warranted to prevent intoxication.

GEN. And now that I've introduced myself, I should like to have some idea of what's going on.
KATE. Oh, Papa-we-
SAM. Permit me, I'll explain in two words: we propose to marry your daughters.
GEN. Dear me!
GIRLS. Against our wills, Papa against our wills!
GEN. Oh, but you mustn't do that! May I ask this is a picturesque uniform, but I'm not familiar with it. What are you?
KING. We are all single gentlemen.
GEN. Yes, I gathered that Anything else?
KING. No, nothing else.
EDITH. Papa, don't believe them; they are pirates the famous Pirates of Penzance!
GEN. The Pirates of Penzance! I have often heard of them.

Gilbert and Sullivan from
The Pirates of Penzance 1879

‹ *Penzance*
Chûn Quoit, West Penwith ›

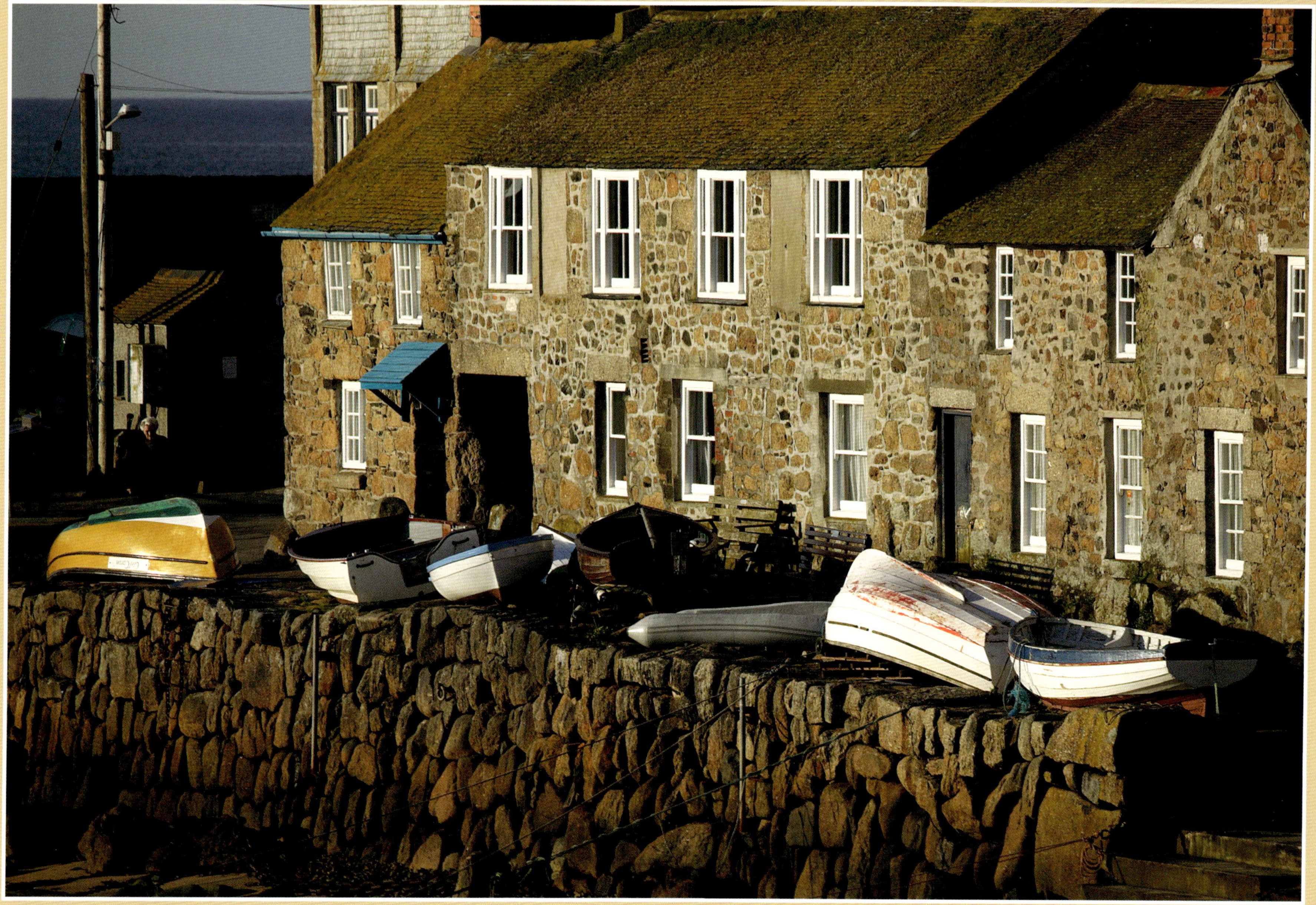

Old Doll Pentreath,
one hundred age and two,
Both born and in Paul parish buried too:
Not in the church 'mongst people great
and high,
But in the church-yard,
doth old Dolly lie.

Epitaph in Paul's churchyard near
Mousehole in both Cornish and English

Mr. Burney called to take me to his house at Mousehole, to which place he had invited me in the kindest manner. Picked up my little baggage and went with him. After dinner went down to the village. Met an old man by the name of James Wright, who took us to the house of a person who had in his possession a large cannon ball, said to have been shot by the Spaniards in old times (1595) against the church of St. Paul. He had also a huge pewter dish which he showed us, bearing the date of 1617. The house put me in mind of a Spanish Galician house. Went thence to visit an old man of eighty, who said that when a boy he had seen Dolly Pentreath of Mousehole, the last person who spoke the Cornish language.

George Borrow 1854

‹ *Mousehole cottages*
   Old granite milestone ›

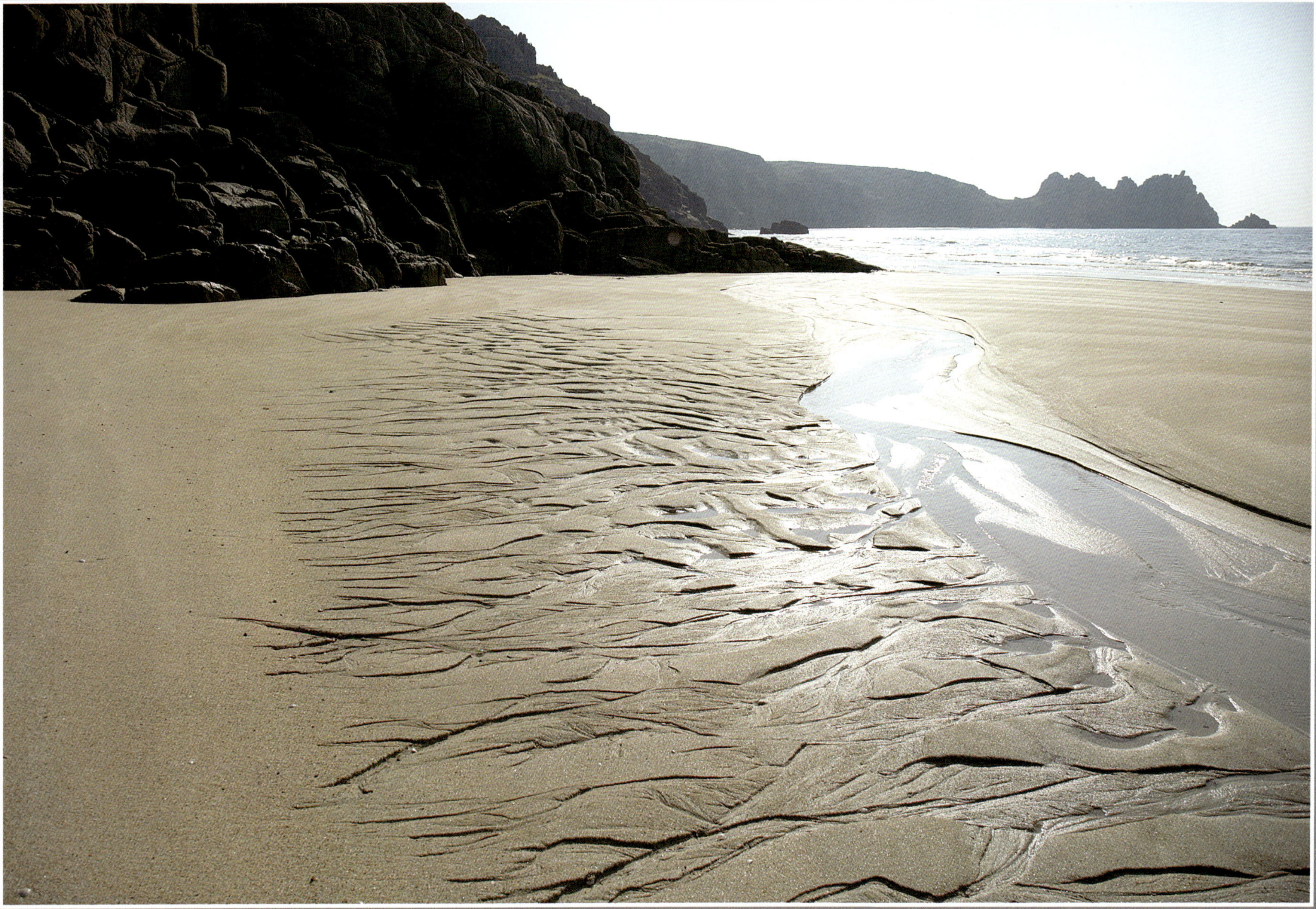

A coming tide, a stretch of gray, wet sand,
A sunset sky, with gold and crimson bright,
Across the sea a rippling path of light.
Weed-covered stones, hollows where clear pools stand,
A crazy boat left lying on the strand.
Low rounded hills that to the sea slope down,
A straggling, whitewashed, little fishing town,
Thin mists of evening creeping o'er the land.
A ridge of wind-blown trees against the sky,
Two women home returning wearily
From mussel-picking; wet with sea and spray,
Bare-legged, with creel on back plodding their way.
Men gazing seaward, leaning on a wall,
Sweet summer twilight brooding over all.

Margaret Ann Courtney 1834-1920

‹ *Porthcurno Beach* ›

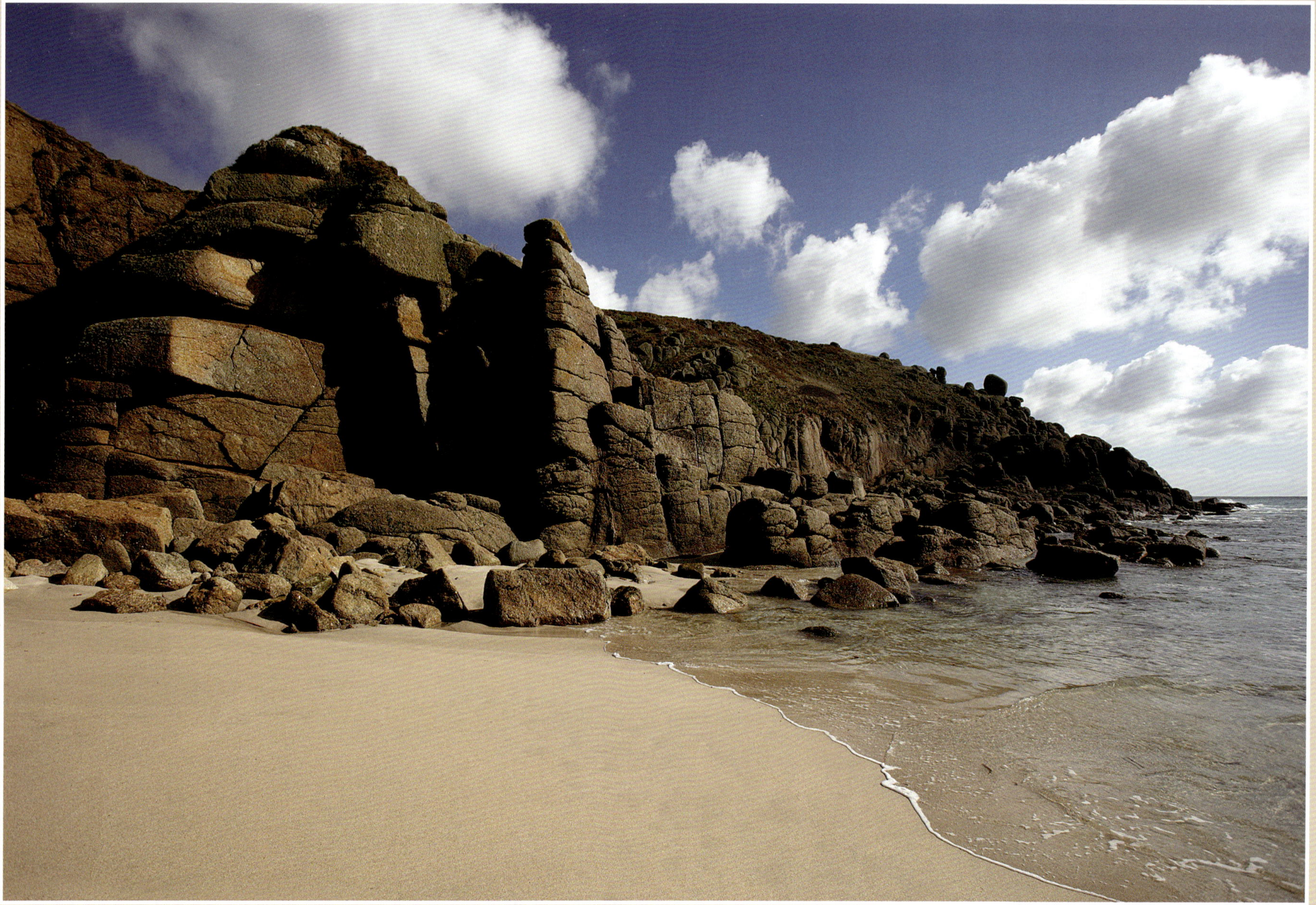

...in retrospect nothing that we had as children made as much difference, was quite so important to us, as our summer in Cornwall....to hear the waves breaking that first night behind the yellow blind; to dig in the sand; to go sailing in a fishing boat; to scrabble over the rocks and see the red and yellow anemones flourishing their antennae; or stuck like blobs of jelly to the rock; to find a small fish flapping in a pool; to pick up cowries;...

Virginia Woolf from Moments of Being 1985

S*he gazed at the sea, trying to decide how, if she were Papa, she would endeavour to paint it. For, although it was blue, it was a blue made up of a thousand different hues. Over sand, shallow and translucent, it was jade-green, streaked with aquamarine. Over rocks and seaweed, it darkened to indigo. Far out, where a small fishing boat bucketed its way across the waves, it became a deep Prussian blue. There was little wind, but the ocean lived and breathed; swelled in from distant depths, formed waves. The sunlight, shining through these as they curved to break, transformed them to moving sculptures of green glass. And, finally, all was drowned in light, that unique suffused brilliance that had first brought the painters to Cornwall, and had driven the French Impressionists into a passion of creativity.*

Rosamunde Pilcher from The Shell Seekers 1987

‹ Porthgwarra Beach
Lifeguard's flag on Sennen Beach ›

*A*s the ground grew higher the great ocean appeared, receiving the universe at evening with is comets, its meteors, nebulae and sunsets as if it were the deep mind held in a sea reflector, forming, as it seemed to me, a timeless clock to record eternity. The long granite cottage was built in a nest of rocks worn by the sea, scooped out by centuries of winds, swirling particles of quartz, flashing felspar. Here Aleister Crowley still lurked. The ghost of D H Lawrence still haunted the plateau below where Frieda sang German songs. A place where anything could happen, built on an ancient burial ground shut in by the solid glass wall of the sea on three sides. It holds things men of the city have forgotten. The men who built the cromlechs in their gigantic simplicity and believed in the vision of our two worlds with an intuitive understanding still moved under the stones.

Sven Berlin from The Coat of Many Colours 1994

❮ *Sea Pinks*
Gurnard's Head ❯

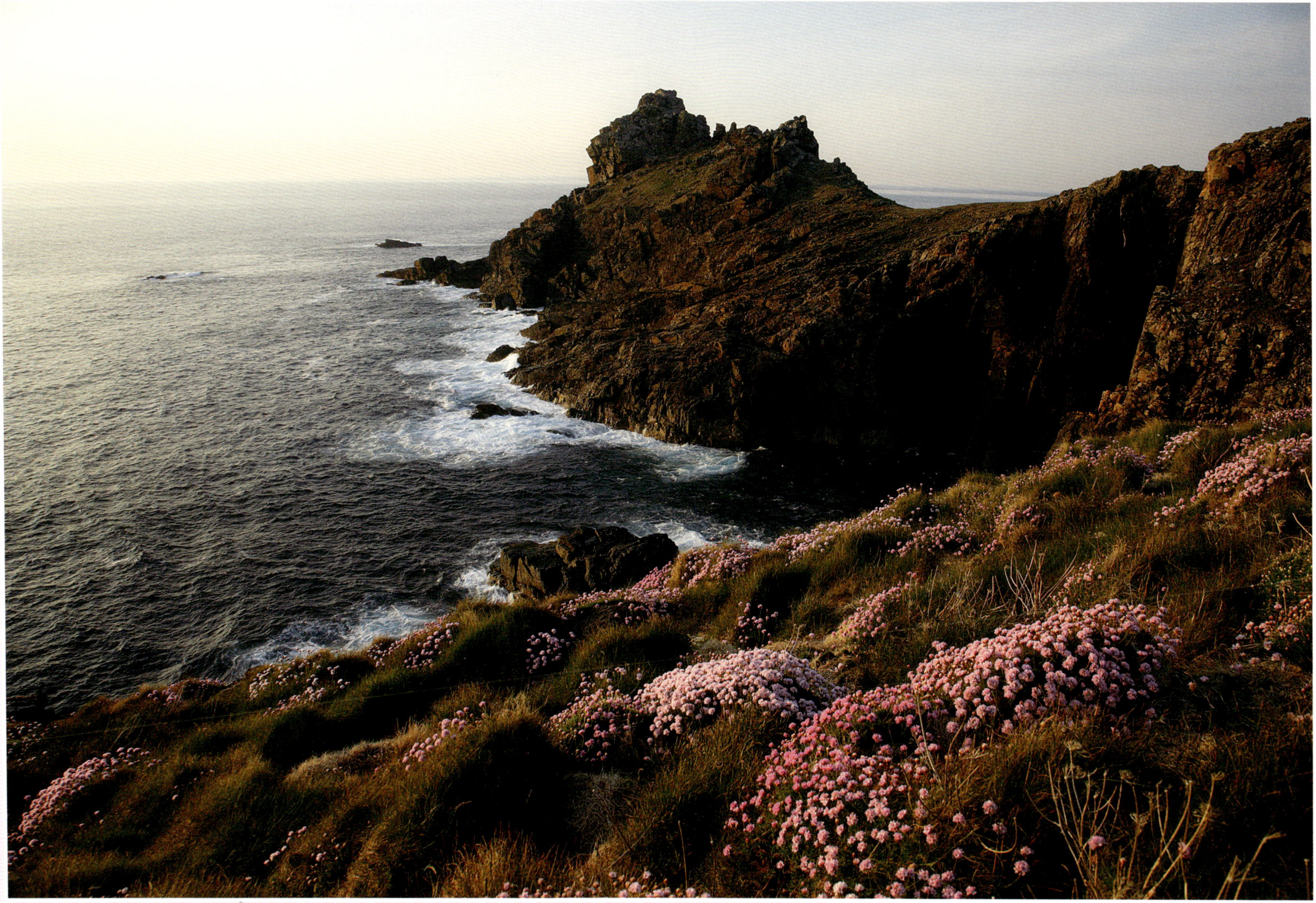

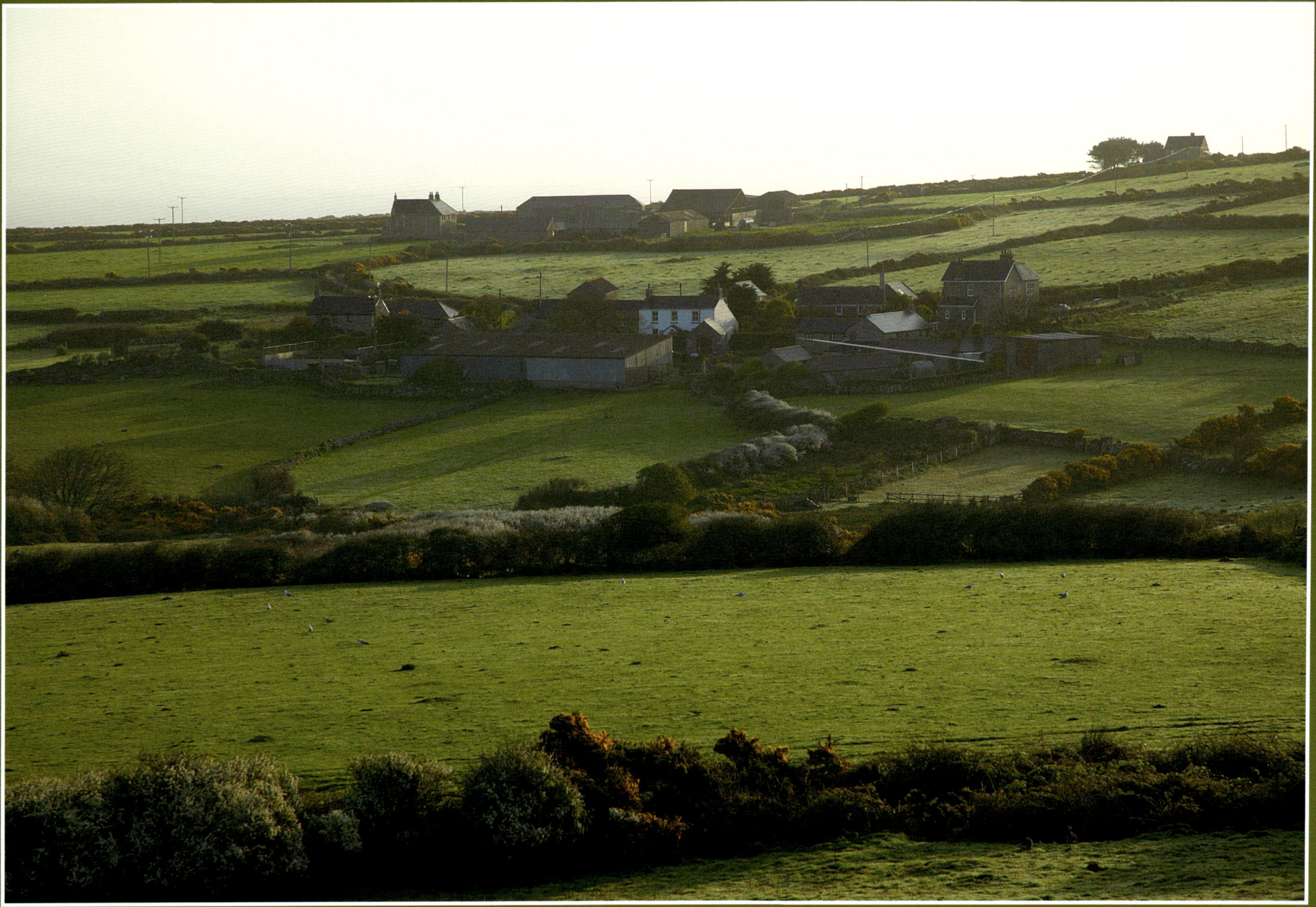

This "Curved form" was conceived standing on the hill called Trevalgan between St Ives and Zennor where the land of Cornwall ends and the cliffs divide as they touch the sea facing west. At this point, facing the setting sun across the Atlantic, where sky and sea blend with hills and rocks, the forms seem to enfold the watcher and lift him towards the sky.

*Barbara Hepworth statement on 'Curved Form'
Holland Park Sculpture Exhibition 1957*

We saw the Land's End, and walked along the coast to the Logan, with a fearful sea rolling at our side. It was magnificent. We went down Botallock mine, which to my mind is as grand as anything I recollect. We have only one more week here. I wish I could stay here longer, it is a delightful neighbourhood and full of interest. Now and then one feels very near the old world. How careless people are about Celtic antiquities; while they send men-of-war to fetch home the lions and bulls of Nineveh, farmers are allowed to pull down cromlechs and caves, and use the stones for pig-styes.

From The Life and Letters of the Right Honourable Friedrich Max Muller 1902

‹ *Farming on the edge of the sea near St Ives*
Carbis Beach ›

All this shoreline, from St Ives to Crantock, is badly affected by the sand, and there is hardly anything of note the whole way.

John Leland's Itinerary   16th century

Always there are fishermen propping up the walls of the Sloop Inn, the haunt of all artists, novelists, and searchers after old wives' tales, waiting for the great moment when the huers shall signal the approach of pilchards in the bay with cries of "Heva! Heva!" Then the seine-boats are launched, the tuck-boats follow, the vast shoal is netted, and all the world of gulls and men collects to see pilchards in the million. Once in the 'forties, seventy-five million were netted in one day, and St Ives was £60,000 the richer.

S P B Mais from The Cornish Riviera   1928

‹ The Island viewed from St Ives cemeterey
St Ives at dawn ›

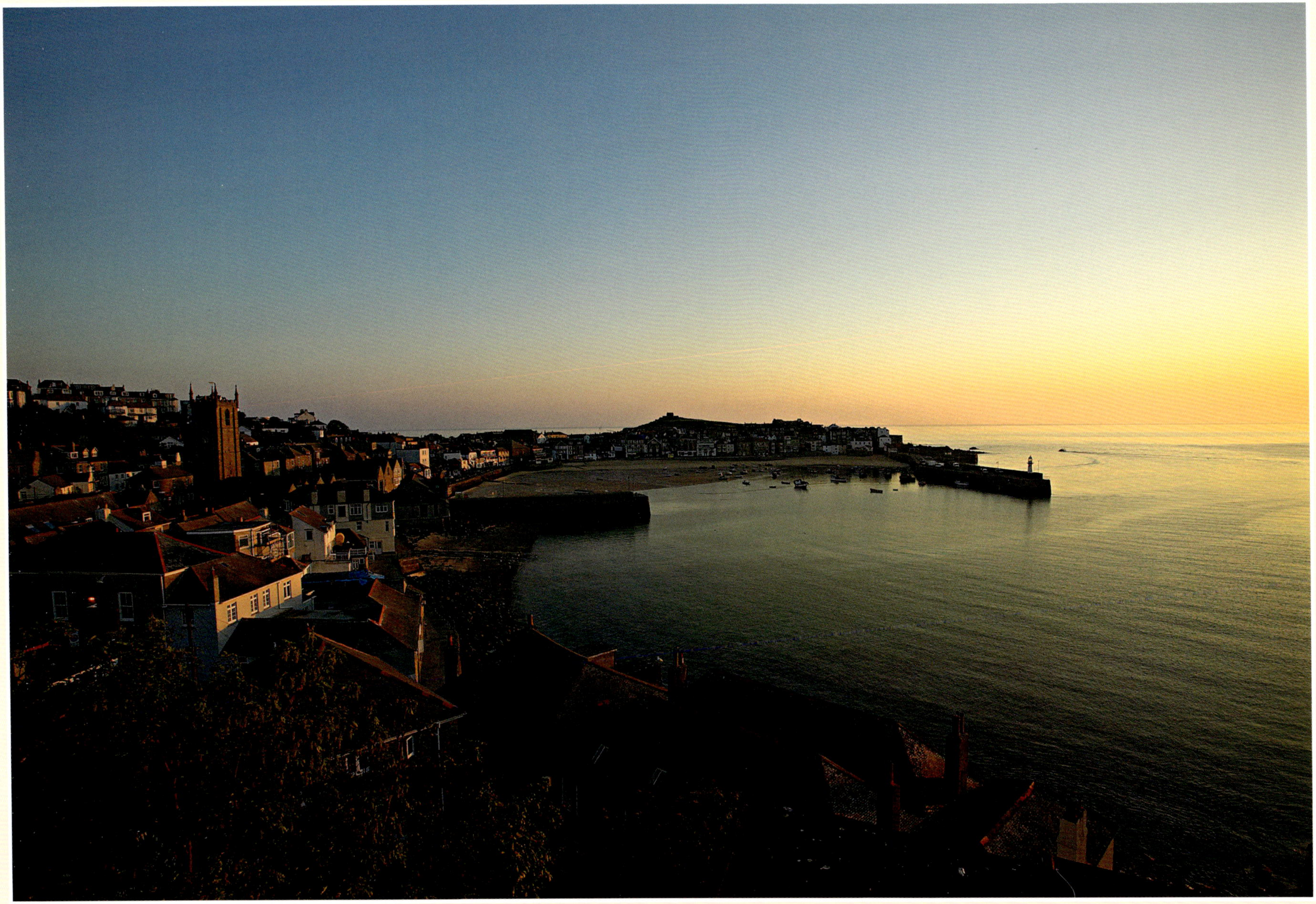

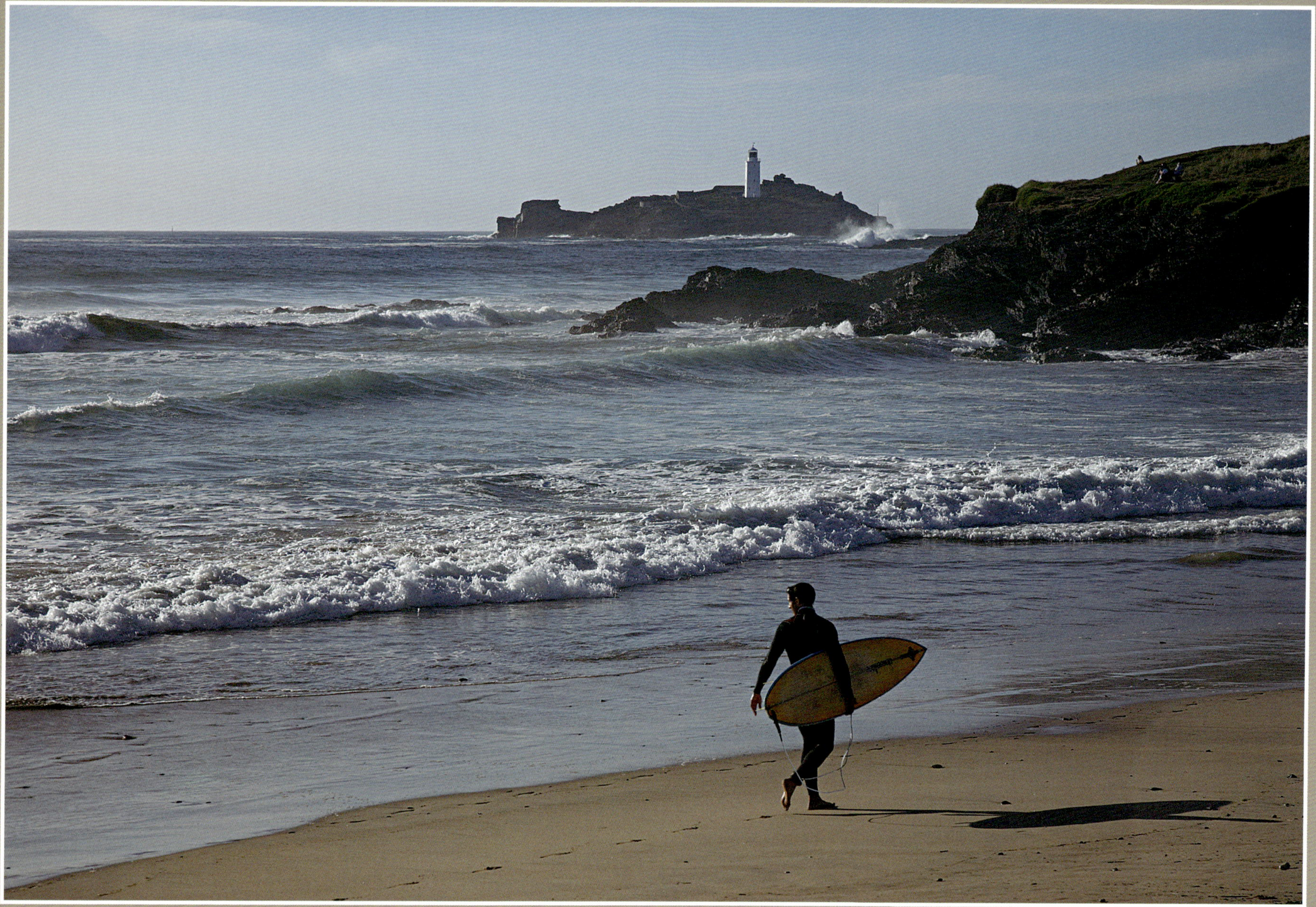

Here was the sublime climate and the pearly light favoured by water-colourists, the sublime bay of St Ives and the sublime lighthouse that inspired Virginia Woolf to write one of her greatest novels, and the sublime charm of the twisty streets and stone cottages.

Paul Theroux from
The Kingdom by the Sea 1984

Almost everywhere else on the English coast the sea is opaque. Here only is it always clear as a diamond, changing in a instant from aqua-marine to peridot, from a blue that is almost purple to a green that is nearly yellow. On no other coast do the waves dash up in long rollers for the surf-board riders to crest, on no other coast are there so many natural diving boards of rock overlooking secluded pools of infinite depth. Nowhere else does the sea make its terrific power felt so strongly. It may be friendly and full of colour to us in the summer, but the churchyards are full of bodies of shipwrecked sailors, masts still emerge from the water at low tide, and skeletons of old ships stand out from wind-blown sands.

S P B Mais from The Cornish Riviera 1928

‹ Surfer on Gwithian Beach with Godrevey Lighthouse behind
Gwithian Beach ›

But both Exeter and Plymouth had been cities of devilment and wild living by comparison with the dripping, granite mining-town far down the Cornish peninsula, with cramped alleys steaming with sea-mist, and stunted trees made hunchback by the gales. The cast was spread round half a dozen guest houses, and Charlie's luck was a slate-gabled island entirely surrounded by hydrangeas, where the drumming of the London bound trains as she lay in bed made her feel like a castaway taunted by the glimpse of distant ships. Their theatre was a rig inside a sports hall, and from its creaking stage she could smell the chlorine from the swimming pool and hear the sluggish thud of squash-balls through the wall.

John le Carré from The Little Drummer Girl   1983

❮ *Dawn at Porthtowan Beach* ❯

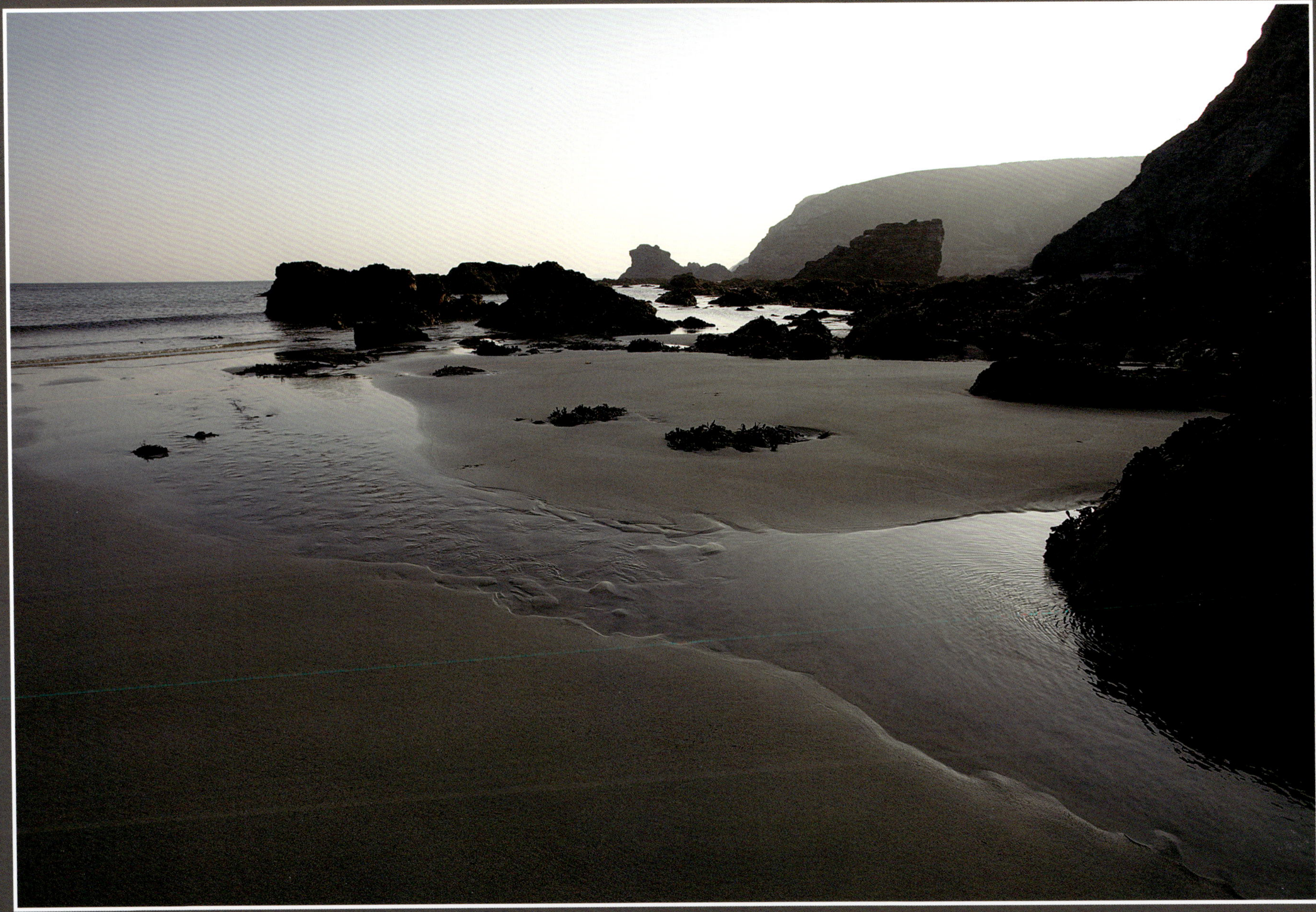

The furze and heather are in bloom,
The moors are fragrant with perfume;
Afar is heard the hum of bees,
Whose murmurs mingle with the trees.
The waters flow the fens among,
The skylark fills the glades with song,
And in the wood where Summer strays
The throstle like a poet plays.
O now to tread some hillock high,
To catch the breeze that murmurs by
From banks of thyme and beds of flowers,
Where Nature rears her own green bowers,
And tunes her harp, and sings for aye
Her soothing everlasting lay!
My Cornwall! what a land is thine
For crag and cross, for moor and mine!

Thy hills are zoned with copper ore;
Thy vales yield tin, a precious store;
The greenest grass thy glades afford;
Thy sheltered bays with fish are stored;
Thy granite carns are castle-crowned,
Where altar-heaps and forts are found.
No brooks are clearer than thine own,
Which steal by cave and cromlech stone;
And every hill-top in the land
Is marked by rude tradition's hand.
Sweet wild-flowers hang their lamps of love
By path below and rift above.
Thy sons are brave, thy daughters fair,
And none can with thy wives compare.

John Harris from A Lay of the Druids 1868

‹ *Early morning at Mawgan Porth*
Watergate Bay ›

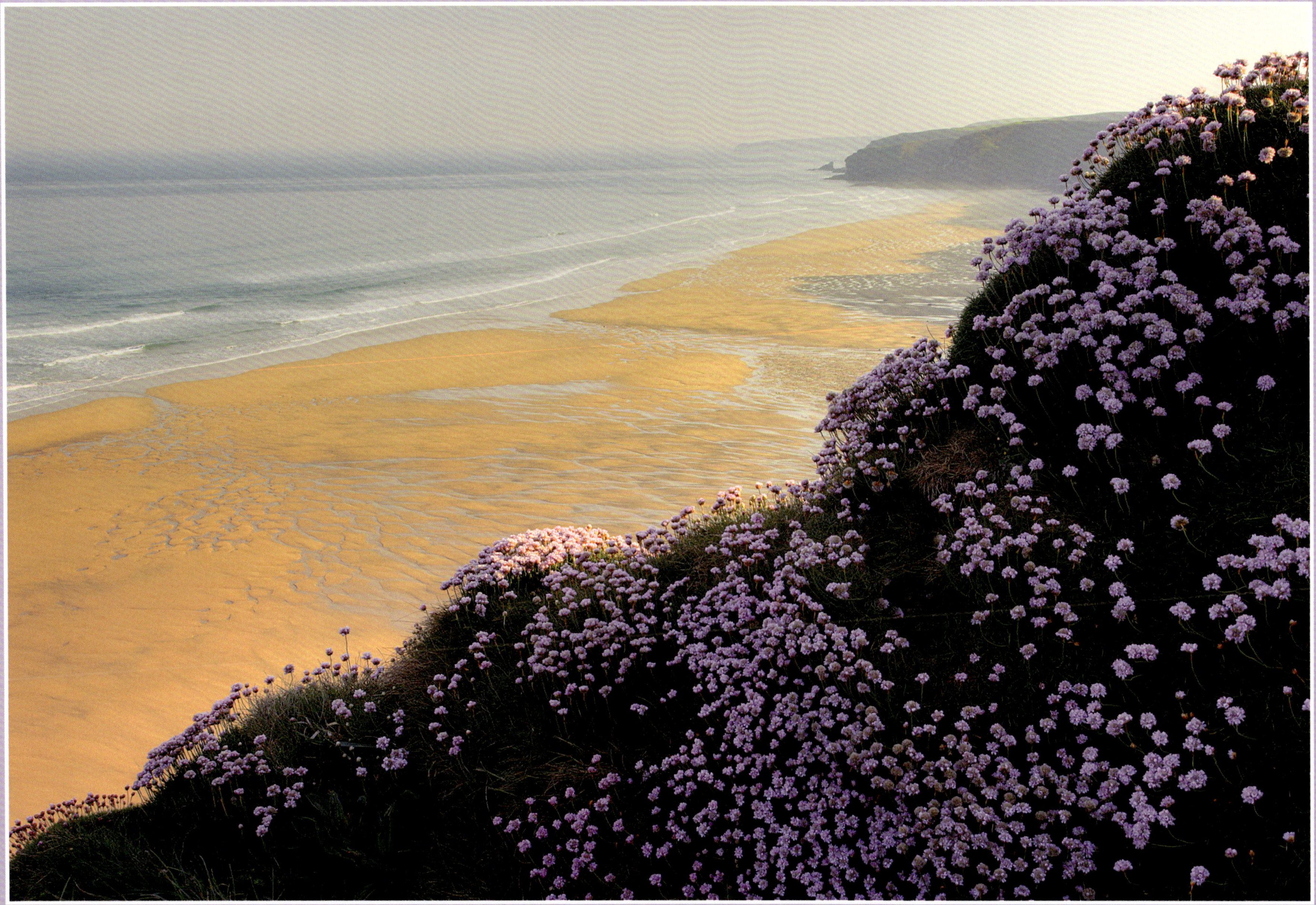

It was a lonely and beautiful place. Wherever Harry went inside the tiny cottage or its garden, he could hear the constant ebb and flow of the sea, like the breathing of some great, slumbering creature. He spent much of the next few days making excuses to escape the crowded cottage, craving the cliff-top view of open sky and wide, empty sea, and the feel of cold, salty wind on his face.

J K Rowling from 'Harry Potter and the Deathly Hallows'   Copyright J K Rowling © 2007

‹ Cornish Hedge
Porthcothan ›

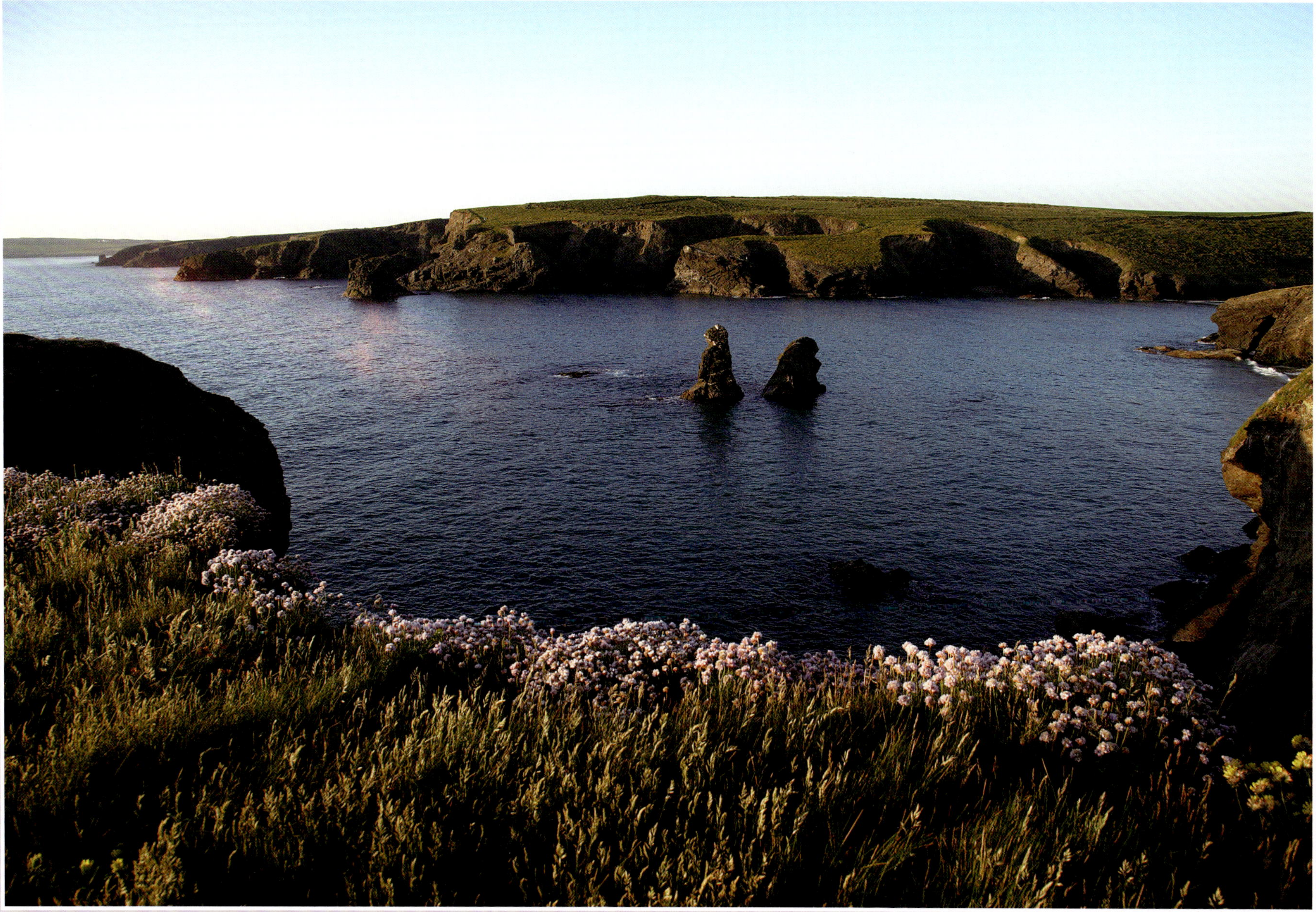

Four miles from Wadebridge is Padstow, a good fishing town, which is busy but dirty. It is an ancient town, called Lodenek in Cornish, but its real English name, according to old documents, is Adelstow, the place of Athelstan...... Many small ships from Brittany come to Padstow to trade in goods from their own country and to buy fish. The town is full of Irishmen.

John Leland's Itinerary   16th century

*T*re, Pol and Pen, Under the influence of these strange names, the peculiarities of the people, and unfamiliar landscape features, it seemed to me more than once that I was in a foreign country, and I caught myself saying in conversation - "When I get back to England".

Walter White from A Londoner's Walk to the Land's End   1855

‹ 'Obby 'Oss day, Padstow
Padstow Harbour ›

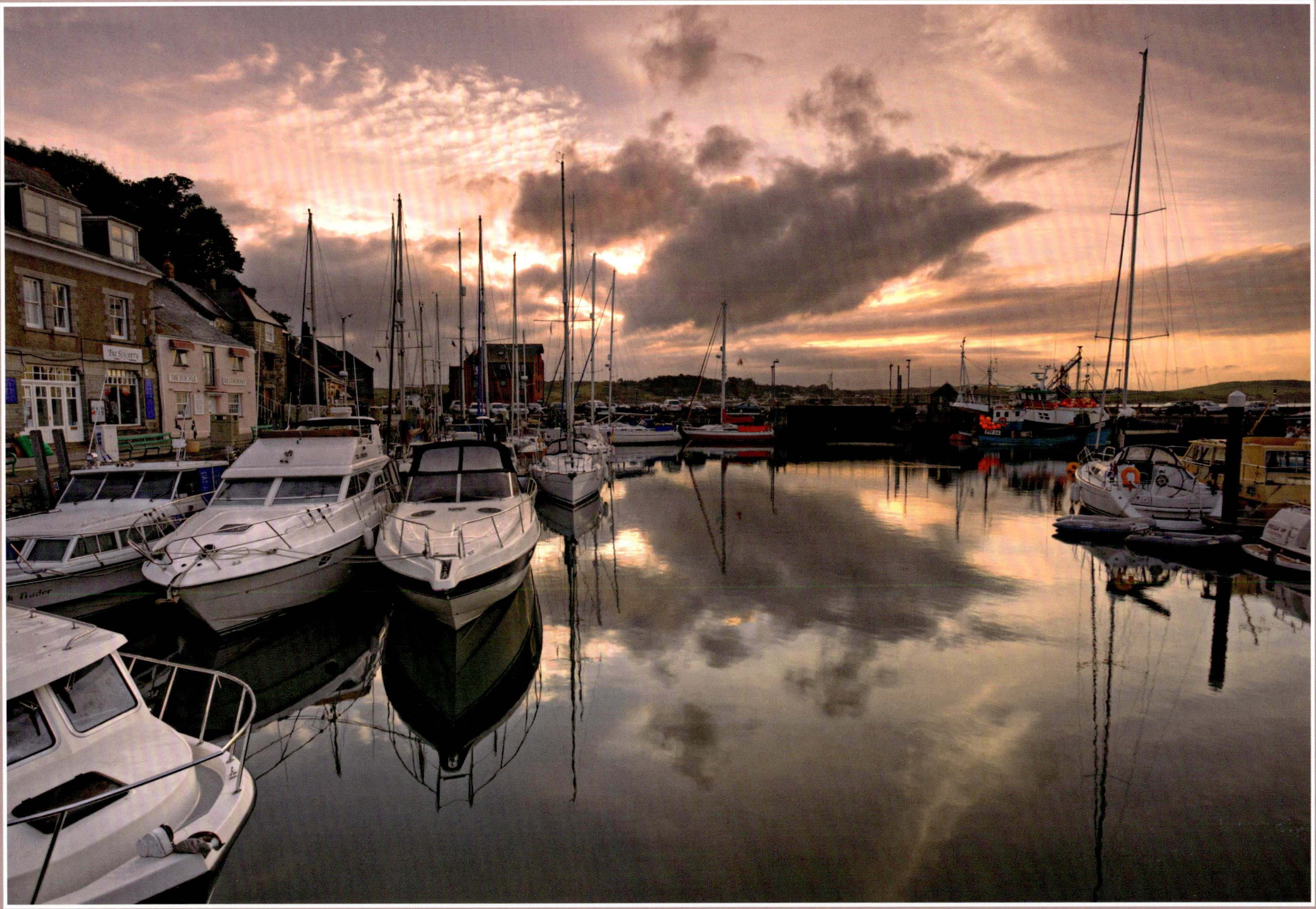

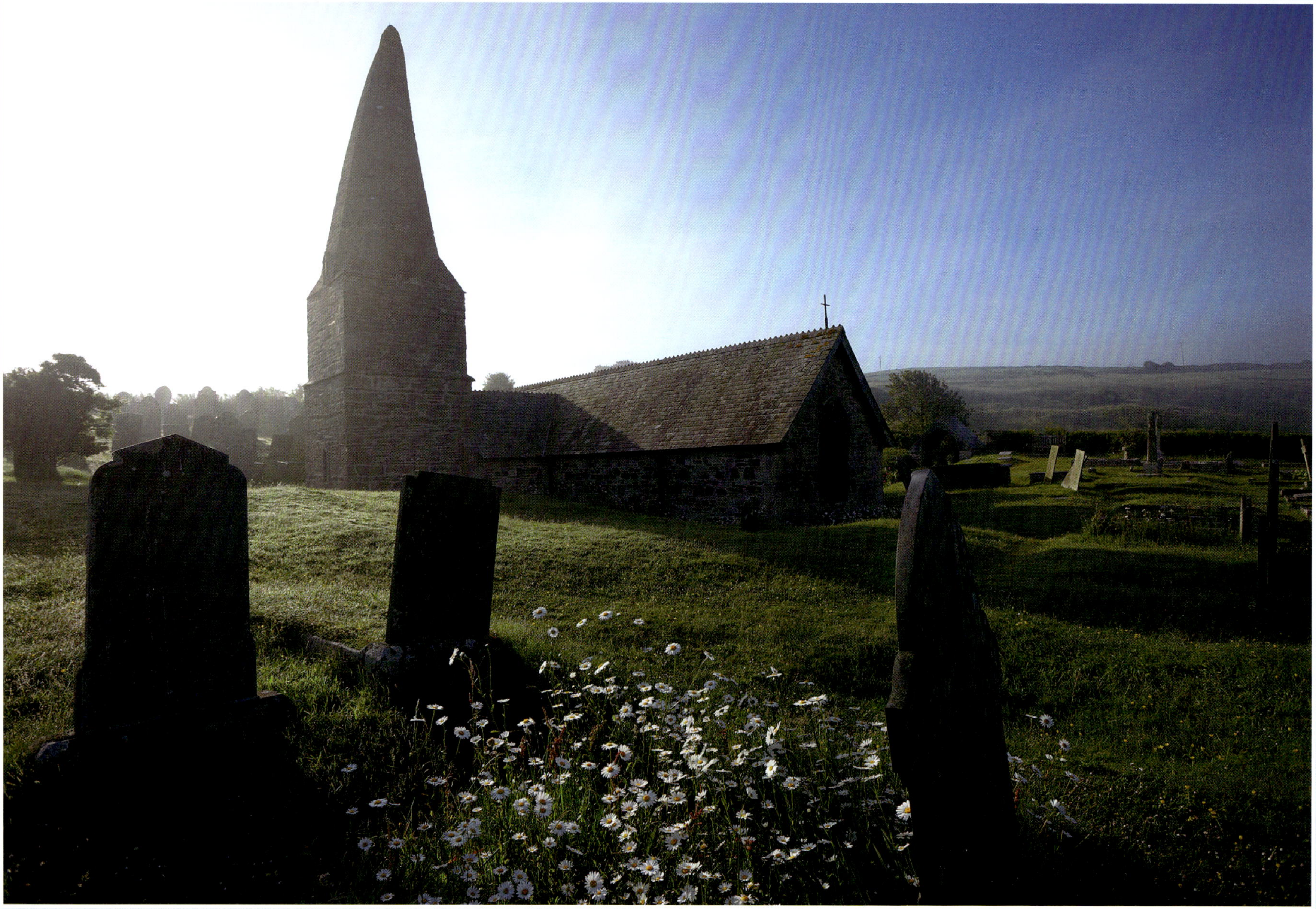

Gwendolen reigned for fifteen years after the death of Locrinus, who had himself reigned ten years. As soon as she realized that her son Maddan had grown to man's estate, she passed the sceptre of the realm to him, being content herself with the province of Cornwall for the remainder of her life.

Geoffrey of Monmouth from The History of the Kings of Britain c 1136

❮ *St Enodoc Church, Daymer Bay, Rock*
  St. Catherine's Church, Temple ❯

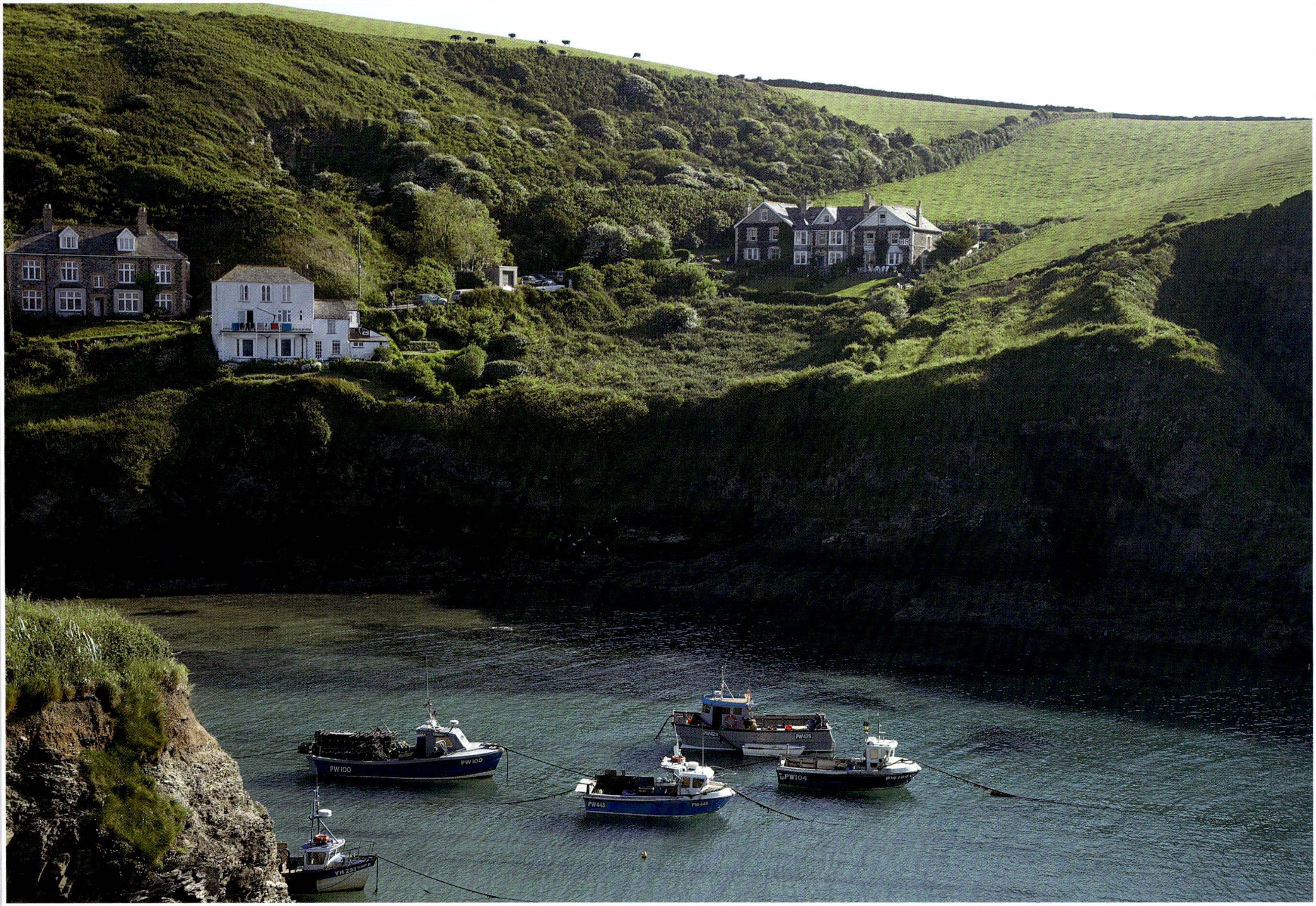

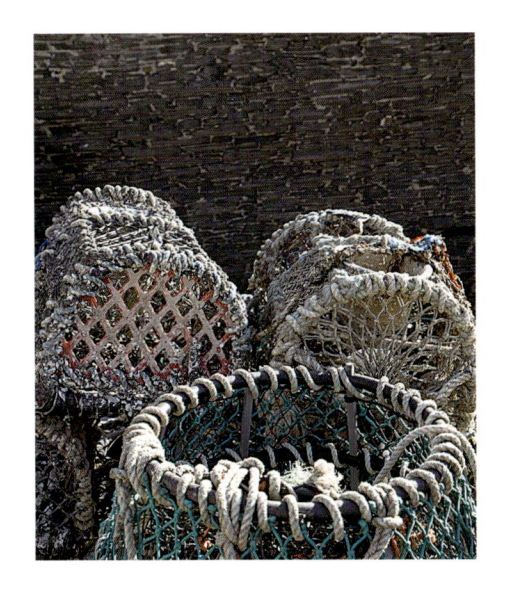

I am perfectly satisfied with Cornwall as it is, and think that it has developed as a holiday resort quite enough. For goodness' sake let us have some place that knows not the tripper - that is innocent even of a 'season's band'. Cornwall is not at present overrun by the former, or rendered melodious by the latter. Long may it remain the happy hunting-ground of those who, like myself, love peace and quietness.

J L W Page from The Cornish Magazine   1898

MRS DUBEDAT [a little cheered] Will you bring the man up here, Mr Walpole, and tell him that he may see Louis, but that he mustnt exhaust him by talking? [Walpole nods and goes out by the outer door]. Sir Ralph, dont be angry with me; but Louis will die if he stays here. I must take him to Cornwall. He will recover there.

B. B. [brightening wonderfully, as if Dubedat were already saved] Cornwall! The very place for him! Wonderful for the lungs. Stupid of me not to think of it before. You are his best physician after all, dear lady. An inspiration! Cornwall: of course, yes, yes, yes.

MRS DUBEDAT [comforted and touched] You are so kind, Sir Ralph. But dont give me much or I shall cry; and Louis cant bear that.

B. B. [gently putting his protecting arm round her shoulders] Then let us come back to him and help to carry him in. Cornwall! of course, of course. The very thing! [They go together into the bedroom].

George Bernard Shaw from The Doctor's Dilemma   1906

‹ Port Isaac
Crab Pots at Port Isaac ›

...the charm of some of the most romantic and sublime scenery in the Empire. Cornwall is the land of the wild, the picturesque and the imaginative.

Cyrus Redding from Illustrated Itinerary of the County of Cornwall 1842

Suddenly, as if some enchanter had waved his wand, the mist lifted and a blaze of sunshine gilded the splendid coastline and crested, with rainbow hues, the great waves. The tide was on the turn and, here and there, were patches of golden sand broken up by black rocks. I felt I must shout, sing or do something to hail such majestic beauty. Instead I stooped, plucked a little sprig of purple ling, and placed it in my coat as a symbol, I suppose, of the eternal romance of this remote western land.

Frederick I Cowles from The Magic of Cornwall 1934

‹ *Cliffside Sea Thrift*
Port Gaverne ›

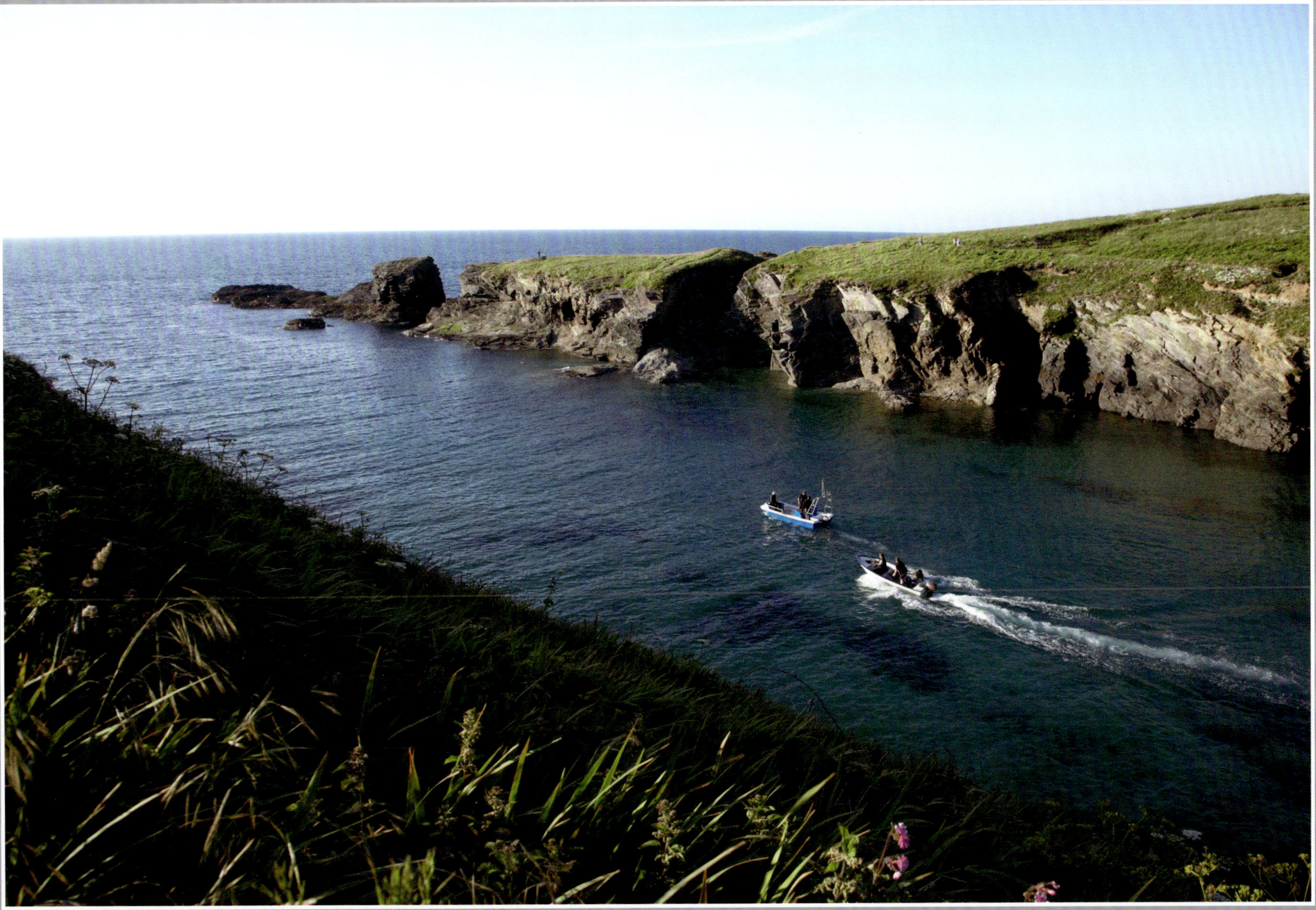

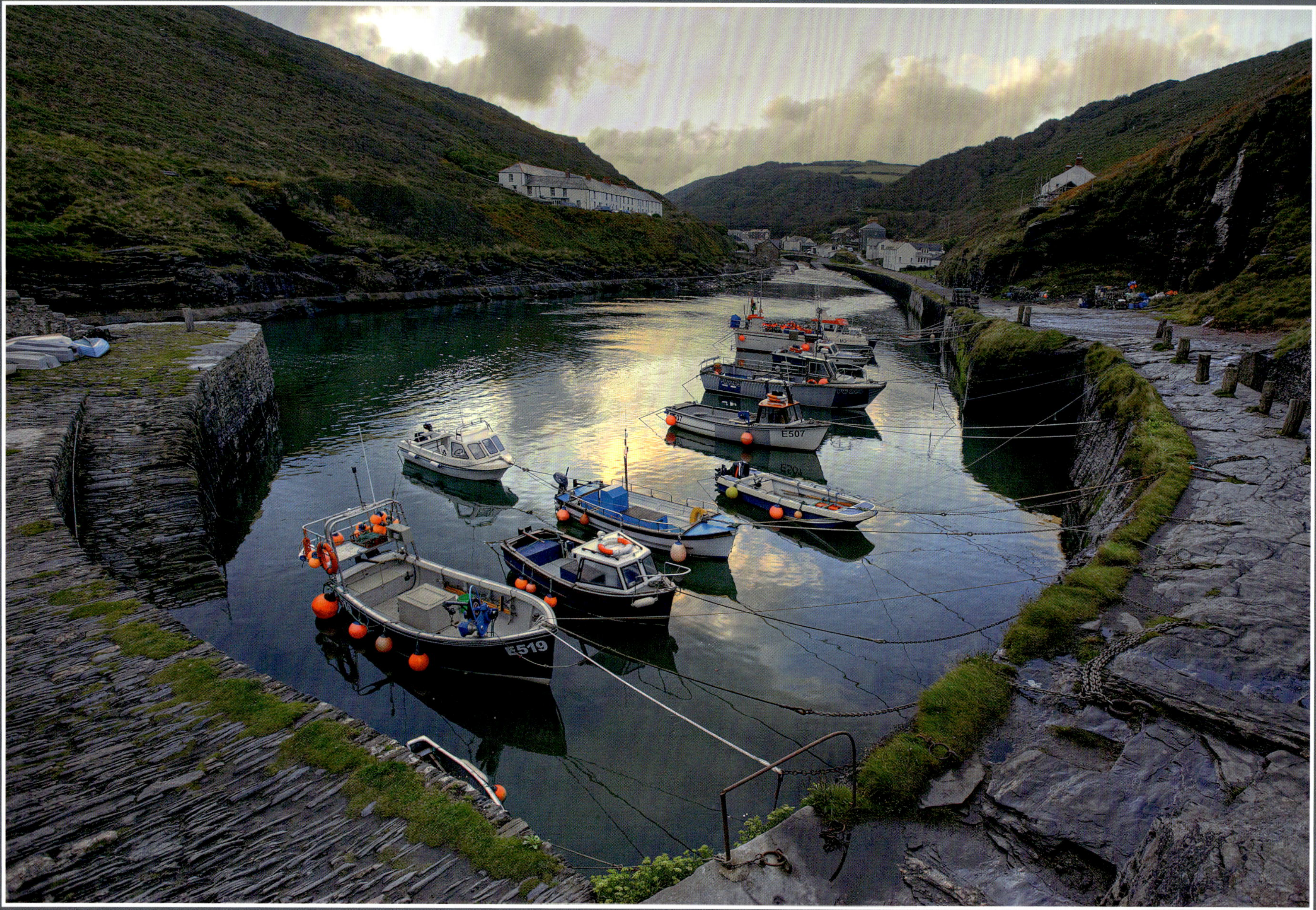
E519
E507

Why go to Saint-Juliot? What's Juliot to me?
　I've been but made fancy
　By some necromancy
　That much of my life claims the spot as its key.

Yes. I have had dreams of that place in the West,
And a maiden abiding
Thereat as in hiding;
Fair-eyed and white-shouldered, broad-browed and brown-tressed.

And of how, coastward bound on a night long ago,
There lonely I found her,
The sea-birds around her,
And other than nigh things uncaring to know.

So sweet her life there (in my thought has it seemed)
That quickly she drew me
To take her unto me,
And lodge her long years with me. Such have I dreamed.

But nought of that maid from Saint-Juliot I see;
Can she ever have been here,
And shed her life's sheen here,
The woman I thought a long housemate with me?

Does there even a place like Saint-Juliot exist?
Or a Vallency Valley
With stream and leafed alley,
Or Beeny, or Bos with its flounce flinging mist?

Boscastle Harbour
　Boscastle Panorama ❯

Thomas Hardy 'A Dream or No' 1913

'Cawk! Cawk!' then said the raven,
'I am fourscore years and ten.
Yet never in Bude Haven
Did I croak for rescued men -

They will save the Captain's girdle,
And shirt, if shirt there be :
But leave the blood to curdle,
For my old dame and me.'

So said the rushing raven,
Unto his hungry mate, --
'Ho! gossip! for Bude Haven:
There be corpses six or eight.
Cawk! cawk! the crew and skipper,
Are wallowing in the sea:
O what a savoury supper,
For my old dame and me.'

Robert Stephen Hawker from the ballad
A Croon on Hennacliff   1869

‹ Bude
Bude Canal lock gates ›

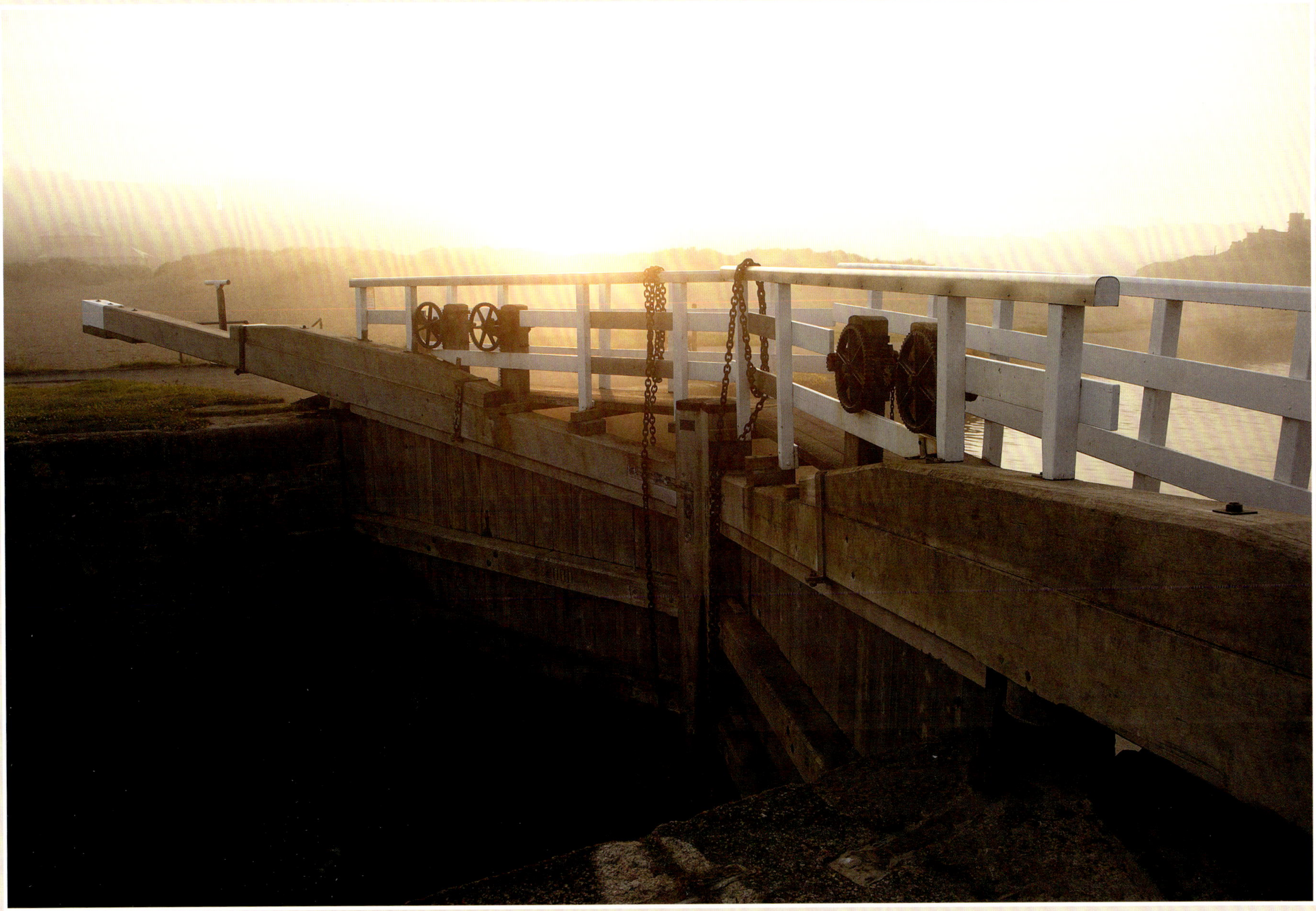

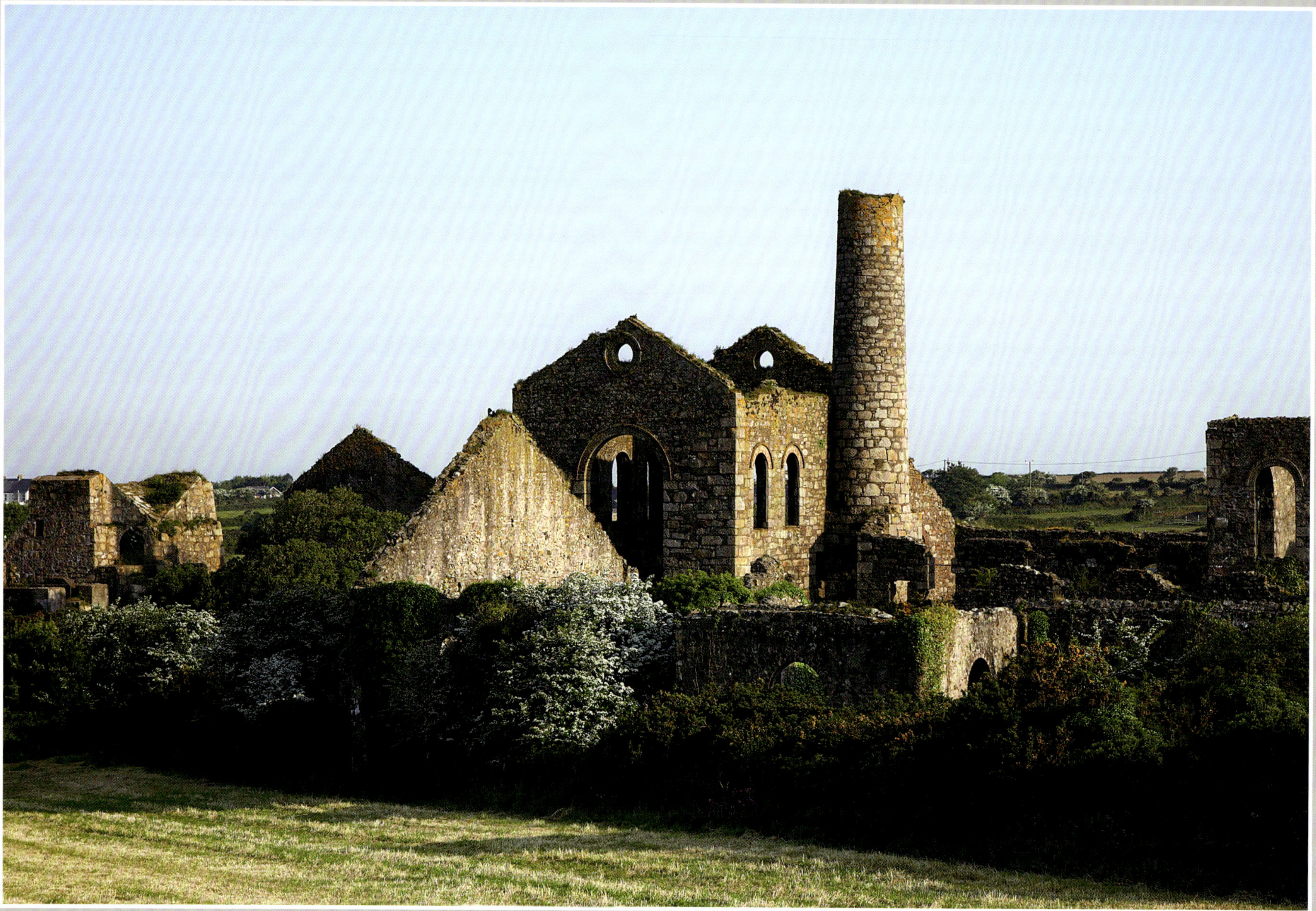

In the Breage mining district....nicknames are very common....generally by way of distinguishing between persons of the same name...16 John Richards's, distinguished by the following additions - Flint, Bustis, Lugger, Roper, Cock, Casley, Tubby, Keel, Shy, Bakester, Rey, Thatcher, Gay, Honey, Jack, Porthlevener and Francis.

From The West Briton newspaper 1883

In no part of England was the preaching of John Wesley more crowned with success than in Cornwall: men who had been eminent for fighting, drinking, and all manner of wickedness, now became eminent for sobriety, piety, and all manner of goodness.

James F Cobb from
The Watcher on the Longships 1876

‹ Old mine workings at the Great Flat Lode
Great Flat Lode in the snow ›

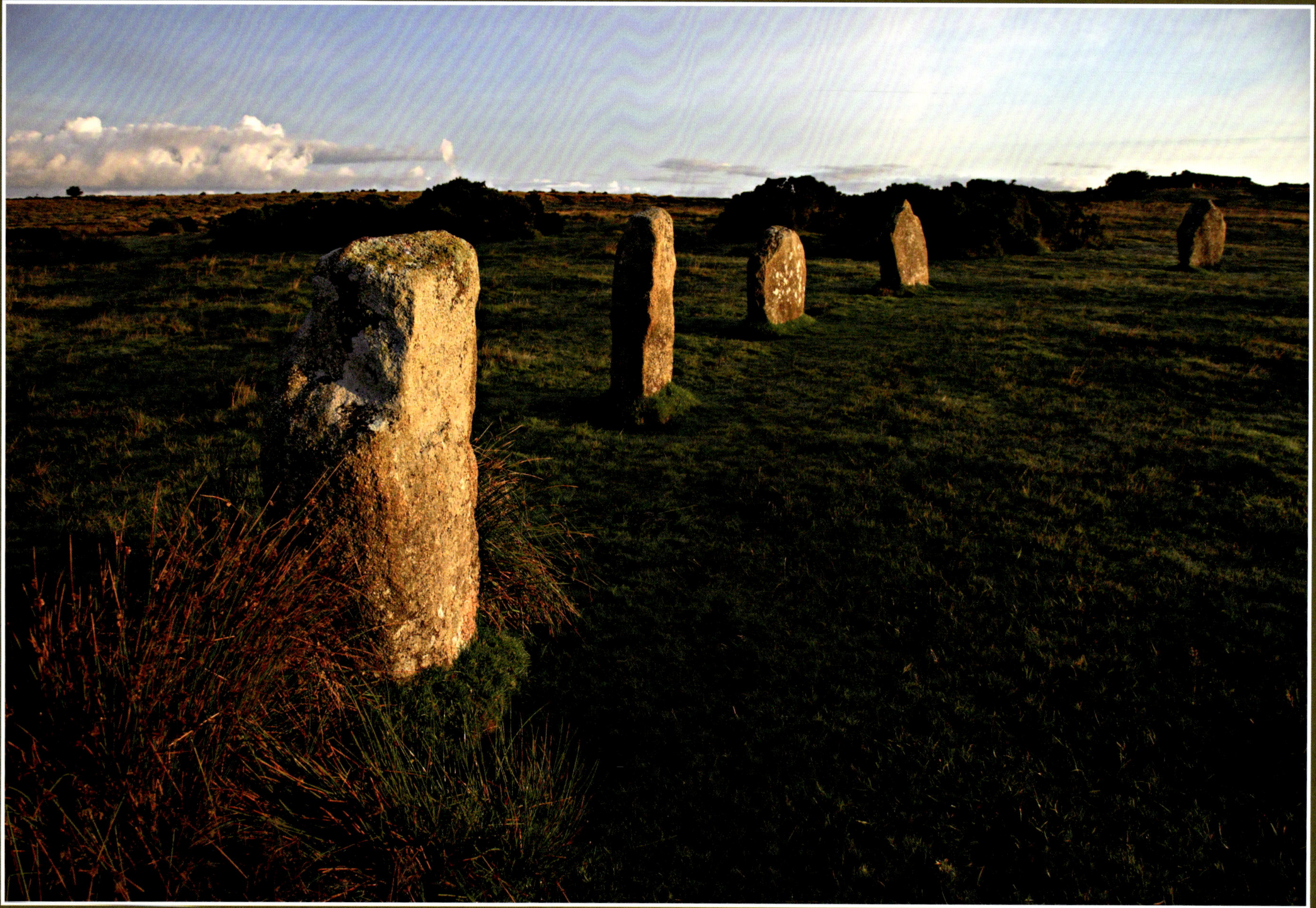

The neighbour Inhabitants terme them Hurlers, as being by a devout and godly error perswaded they had beene men sometimes transformed into Stones for profaning the Lords Day with hurling the ball.

William Camden from Britannia 1610

Why should Cornishmen learn Cornish? There is no money in it, it serves no practical purpose...The question is a fair one, the answer is simple. Because they are Cornish.

Henry Jenner from
Handbook of the Cornish Language 1904

‹ The Hurlers, Minions
Early morning at the Hurlers ›

Afterwards ascended Carn Brea. The Carn is composed of six or seven grey stones pointing N.E. and S.W. They look like huge rhinoceroses piled upon one another. On the top of the Carn there are two little basins about seven feet from each other; three mysterious little holes about the diameter of a penny seem to have connected them. Written on the top of the sacrificial rock. In the principal basin--the horrid place of sacrifice--there are outlets for the blood to stream down. There seem to be about eight basins in all.

George Borrow from his diary 1854

COUSIN JACK

This land is barren and broken
Scarred like the face of the moon
Our tongue is no longer spoken
Towns all around face ruin
Will there be work in New Brunswick
Will I find gold in the Cape
If I tunnel way down to Australia
Oh will I ever escape

Where there's a mine or a hole in the ground
That's what I'm heading for that's where I'm bound
So look for me under the lode and inside the vein
Where the copper the clay the arsenic and tin
Run in your blood and under your skin
I'll leave the county behind I'm not coming back
Follow me down cousin Jack

Written by Steve Knightley of the band
Show of Hands   2007

‹ Carn Brea Castle
Altarnun ›

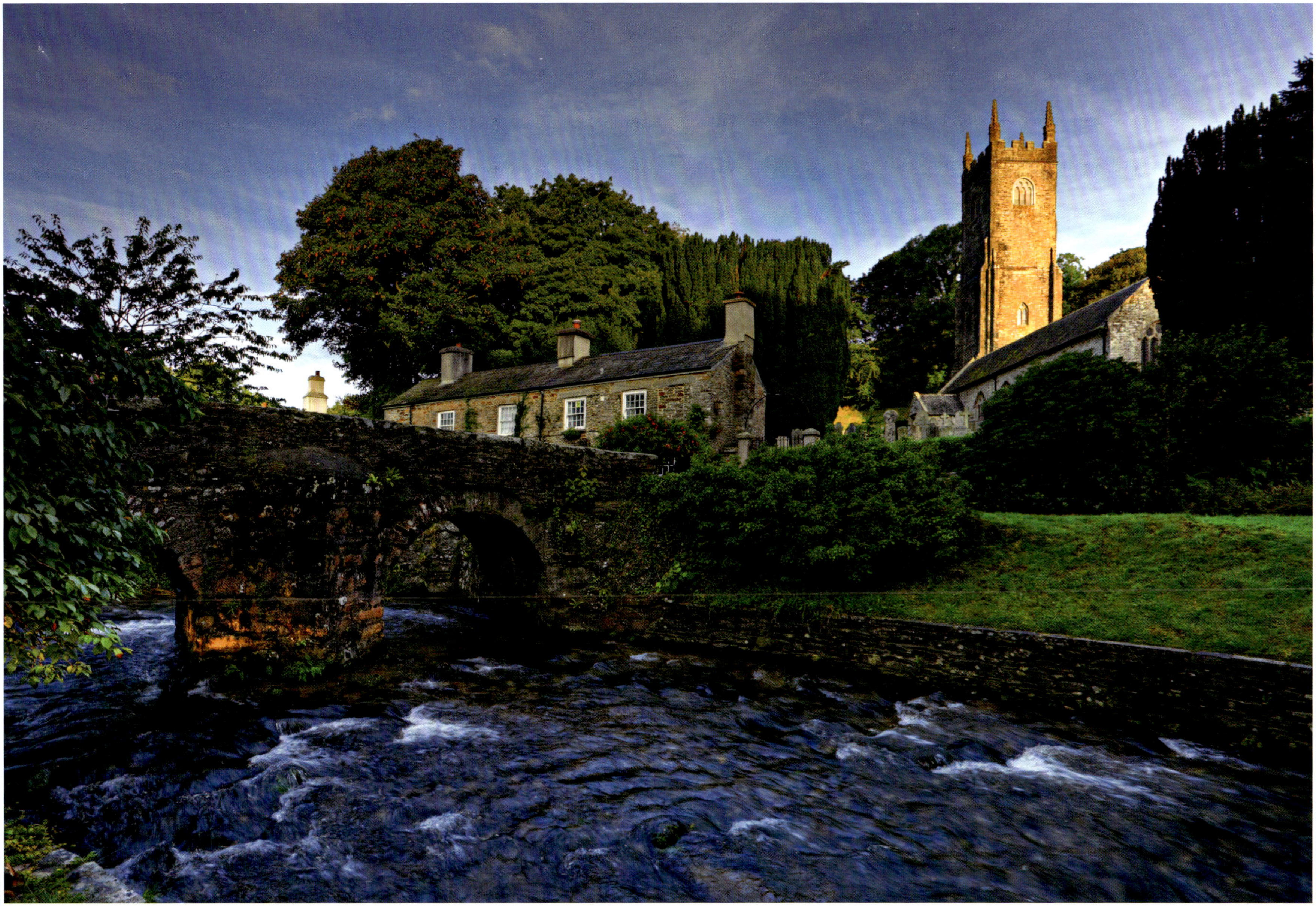

*T*he County of Cornwall forms the western extremity of England. It is surrounded by the British Channel on the north, south, and west sides, and bounded on the east by the County of Devon. It is about 78 miles in length from east to west, and in breadth, next Devonshire, about 43 1/4 miles. This breadth, however, diminishes very rapidly from its eastern boundary towards the Land's End; so that between Mount's Bay and St Ives it is not more than about five miles and a half. The medium breadth may possibly be about 20 miles. The circumference of the county is computed to be 210 miles, and it contains about 780,500 acres, nine hundreds, 161 parishes, 27 market towns, 14,400 houses, and 188,269 inhabitants. It pays eight parts towards the land-tax, and raises 640 militia. There is a tradition that a large tract of land, called the Lioness, a part of the county connecting it with the Scilly Islands, was at some very remote period swallowed up by the ocean.

Topography of Great Britain by George Alexander Cooke 1805

‹ *The Eden Project* ›

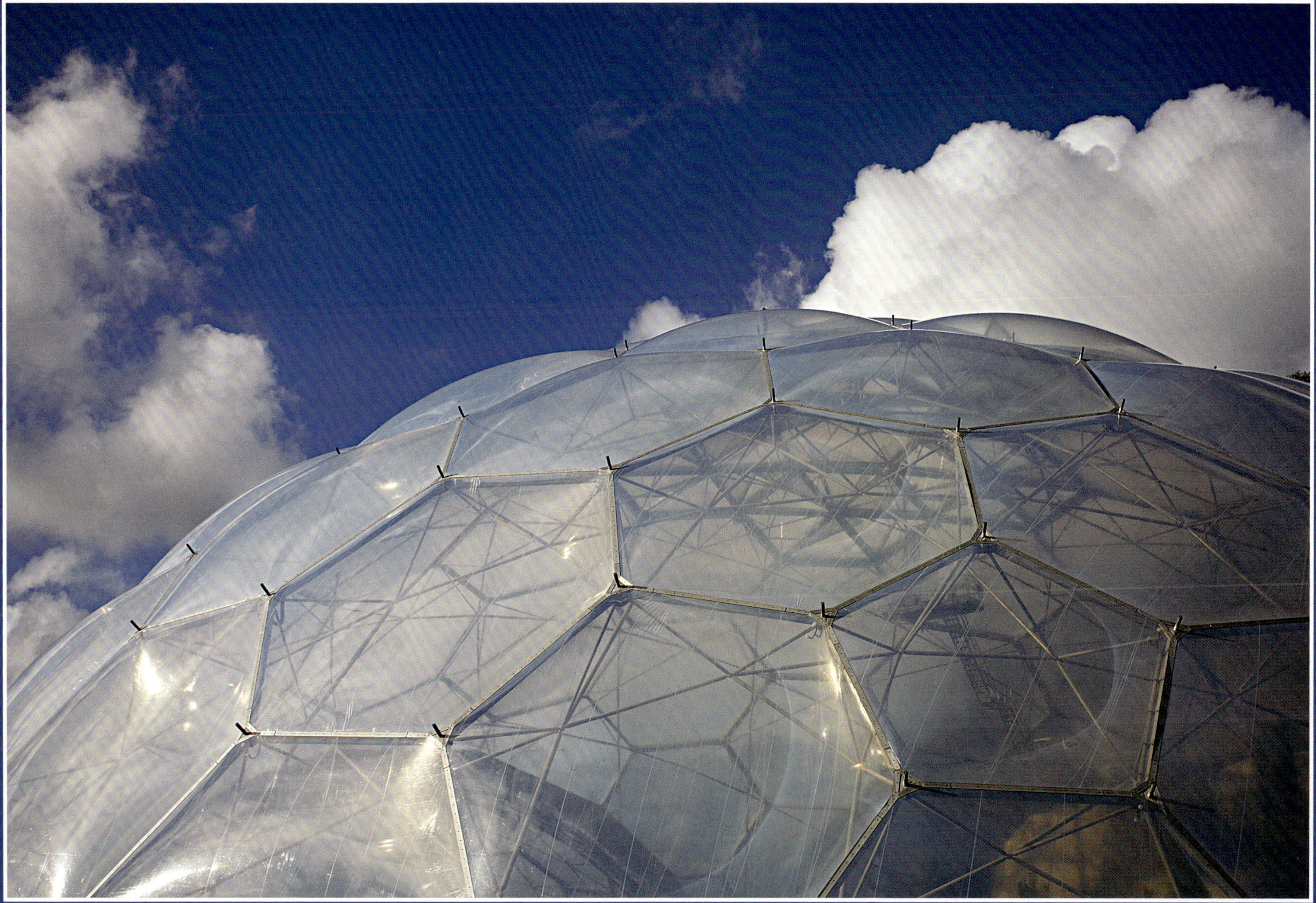

CAPTIONS

Title Page: PORTHTOWAN

The sandy beaches and dunes (towans) have ensured Porthtowan's popularity as a seaside resort since Victorian times. Very popular with surfers, Porthtowan hosts a number of surfing festivals throughout the year.

Frontispiece: TREEN

The path from Treen leads over the cliffs to the rugged and wild Treen Castle and the famous Logan Rock. Pednevounder beach is reached by a steep scramble down the cliff side.

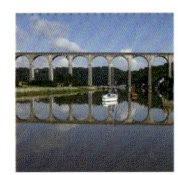

10. CALSTOCK VIADUCT

Lying in the heart of the Tamar Valley the village of Calstock clings to the steep Cornish bank of the River Tamar. It is dominated by the elegant railway viaduct, built in 1908 and carrying the branch line from Plymouth to Gunnislake.

11. THE ROYAL ALBERT BRIDGE

Isambard Kingdom Brunel's famous bridge rises out of the morning mist. Spanning the River Tamar between Plymouth and Saltash, it was opened in 1859 and is the only suspension bridge of its type to carry main line trains.

12. THE SQUARE IN CAWSAND

Located on the 'forgotten' Rame Peninsula five miles from Saltash, Cawsand is a quiet little village of narrow streets and picturesque cottages. The Cawsand ferry links Kingsand and Cawsand to the Barbican in Plymouth, five minutes across the Sound.

13. KINGSAND

The unspoilt fishing village of Kingsand with its colourful painted houses on the Rame Peninsula once, together with its twin village of Cawsand, ran the largest smuggling fleet in Cornwall. Now it is a quiet and peaceful place.

14. LOOE

The picturesque fishing town of Looe is in fact made up of the two villages of East and West Looe which scramble along each side of a steep-sided valley and are connected by a Victorian seven-arched bridge over the River Looe. A small fleet of fishing boats return their catches to the port daily and the town has a reputation for producing excellent fresh fish. Busy and bustling, East Looe's charming narrow streets lead down to a sandy beach and the town's famous Banjo Pier.

16. POLPERRO

Undoubtedly one of the most beautiful villages in Cornwall, Polperro nestles in its cliff ravine and is a picturesque jumble of colour-washed cottages and steeply narrow streets which tumble down to the small harbour. Once a centre for the area's smuggling industry, Polperro still boasts a small fishing fleet and colourful boats are moored in the protected inner harbour.

18. GRAZING ON PENCARROW HEAD

The coastline between Looe and Fowey is dominated by Pencarrow Head. On a clear day you can seen from Rame Head to the Lizard.

19. ST WYLLOW, LANTEGLOS-BY-FOWEY

The 'valley' church of St Wyllow has been the parish church of Lanteglos-by-Fowey since the 15th century. Surrounded on three sides by water, this stunning and remote church is where Daphne du Maurier was married.

20. POLRUAN

The remoteness of the ancient fishing village of Polruan which faces Fowey at the mouth of the river gives the area its unspoilt charm. Its narrow streets and alleyways twist between white-washed cottages, down the steep hill to the sea.

21. FOWEY

A busy, sheltered deep-water small port, Fowey meanders along the banks of the river Fowey, cottages clinging to the hill side. Daphne du Maurier lived at nearby Bodinnick and the eponymous festival is a popular May-time event.

22. MEVAGISSEY

The traditional fishing village of Mevagissey has a colourful history of boat building and smuggling. The unspoilt old centre consists of very narrow picturesque streets full of interesting shops and restaurants. Feast Week is celebrated at the end of June culminating in a carnival and firework display. Although tourism has replaced fishing as the dominant industry in the village, 63 fishing vessels are still registered as working out of Mevagissey harbour.

24. THE SWEEPING HARBOUR AT CHARLESTOWN

Local landowner, Charles Rashleigh, built the Georgian new town of Charlestown to service the thriving copper and china clay industries. Today it is still a working port and is also home to a collection of 'tall ships' which are frequently used in film projects.

25. THE KING HARRY FERRY

One of only 5 chain ferries in the country, the King Harry Ferry carries cars and passengers across the River Fal between Feock and the Roseland Peninsula. Lying on the Pilgrims' Way to St Michael's Mount, a ferry crossing has existed here for centuries.

26. THE TRURO RIVER AT MALPAS

Malpas lies a mile outside the city of Truro where the Rivers Truro and Tresillian converge. It is still a port and is the departing and landing point for boat trips to Falmouth at low tide. Legend has it that Iseult crossed the river here to King Mark's palace.

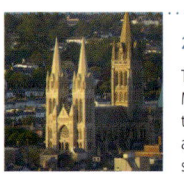

27. TRURO CATHEDRAL SOARS OVER THE CITY

The three spires of the Cathedral of the Blessed Virgin Mary soar over the skyline of Cornwall's only city. It was the first cathedral built in Britain since the Middle Ages and construction in the Gothic Revival architectural style began in 1880.

29. THE RUINED CHURCH AT OLD KEA

The ruined medieval tower of Old Kea Church reaches up out of the tree tops. The small and peaceful chapel is said to be named after the 5th century British Saint Kea and a monastery on this site is mentioned in the Domesday book.

29. COMBE

The hamlet of Combe lies along the banks of the tranquil waters of Cowlands Creek, a tributary of the River Fal, just south of Truro.

30. FALMOUTH

The town of Falmouth was created by Sir John Killigrew shortly after 1613 and received its Royal charter in 1661. Its famous harbour is the third deepest natural harbour in the world and the deepest in Western Europe. The Falmouth Packet Service operated between 1689 and 1851 carrying mail to and from Britain's growing empire. Falmouth is still a cargo port and the docks are a major contributor to the town's economy but it is now primarily a tourist destination particularly for boating and water sports pursuits.

32. THE WATERFRONT VILLAGE OF HELFORD

The picture perfect village of Helford lies on the banks of a sheltered tidal creek, a tributary of the beautiful River Helford. Once a popular haunt of pirates and freetraders, Daphne du Maurier's romantic novel Frenchman's Creek is set in its wooded valleys and along its misty banks. A medieval ferry crossing allows walkers on the coastal path around the Lizard to continue their journey towards Falmouth.

34. COVERACK

The village of Coverack lies on the eastern side of the Lizard Peninsula. Houses tumble down the hill to the sweeping bay and the tiny harbour with its wall made of local hornblende and serpentine stone. The large beach make it perfect for watersports.

35. THE FISHING VILLAGE OF CADGWITH

One of Cornwall's loveliest villages, the naturally protected cove at Cadgwith is still home to a small fleet of fishing boats which are winched up the shingle beach. Thatched cottages tumble down the valley to Cadgwith's two beaches.

36. COASTAL PATH

The 630 mile South West Coast Path rounds the southern most point in the UK on the Lizard Peninsula. The narrow path clings to the cliffside and is lined with colourful wild flowers.

37. KYNANCE COVE

White sand, turquoise water, unique serpentine rock formations and a stunning location, Kynance Cove on the Lizard Peninsula is a famous beauty spot.

38. GUNWALLOE CHURCH COVE

Church bells ring out across the beach from the uniquely placed church at Gunwalloe. The 15th century church of St Winwaloe is set amongst the sand dunes at Gunwalloe Church Cove at the eastern tip of Mounts Bay.

40. WHEAL PROSPER

The not very prosperous Wheal Prosper tin mine in its stunning position overlooking Rinsey Cove, only traded for a short time between 1860-1866.

41. PORTHLEVEN

The sheltered harbour at Porthleven was constructed as a safe haven on this forbidding lee shore. Facing southwest, directly into the prevailing winds the port is well-known for its winter storms and good surfing.

42. ST MICHAEL'S MOUNT

One of England's most famous and dramatic attractions, St Michael's Mount is a tidal island rising out of the seas of Mount's Bay. Owned by the St Aubyn family access is controlled by the National Trust and, of course, the tide!

43. ST MICHAEL'S MOUNT (cont.)

Visitors can walk across the causeway which links the island to Marazion at low tide. Regular ferry services run at high tide. The medieval castle and chapel are open to the public.

44. PENZANCE

Penzance or 'holy headland' in Cornish is the main town of the Land's End Peninsula. Its busy harbour is home to many yachts and pleasure boats and the Isles of Scilly ferry, Scillonian III, sails regularly from here to the Islands.

45. CHÛN QUOIT

High up on the West Penwith moors near Chûn Castle this neolithic dolmen or quoit has a distinct domed capstone. It gets its name from Cornish 'Chy-an-Woone' which means 'The house on the downs.'

46. MOUSEHOLE

The picturesque fishing village of Mousehole nestles around the harbour which protects it from the worst of the winter gales. With narrow streets, twisting alleys and brightly painted cottages, Mousehole is a popular place to visit.

47. ROADSIDE SIGNPOST

In early spring daffodils grow everywhere in Cornwall. Roadside verges, such as this one just outside Mousehole are a riot of nodding yellow flowers.

48. PORTHCURNO BEACH

Porthcurno Beach is a beautiful sweep of white sand and turquoise sea overlooked by the world famous Minack Theatre. The nearby cliffs rise 60-70m and the views from the coastal path are amongst some of the most visually stunning in the south west. In the late 19th century Porthcurno Beach became internationally famous as the British termination of early submarine telegraph cables. The award-winning Porthcurno Telegraph Museum is found close by.

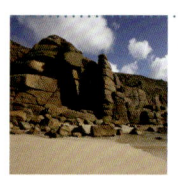

50. PORTHGWARRA

The delightful, secluded cove of Porthgwarra lies 3 miles southeast of Land's End. Once a busy fishing cove, now just one boat regularly works crab pots here. A superb stop off point on the coastal path.

51. SENNEN COVE

The crescent shaped bay at Sennen Cove boasts one of the loveliest stretches of sand - Whitesands Beach. Catching both northerly and southerly swells, it is very popular with surfers. Legend has it that the cove was once heavily populated by mermaids.

52. GURNARD'S HEAD

Located on the rugged north coast near the village of Zennor, the high narrow headland of Gurnard's Head is a magical place. The narrowest part of the promontory has the remains of an ancient defensive ditch and bank wall. Evidence of a tin mine and pilchard works can also be found here.

54. NEAR ST IVES

The agricultural landscape of West Penwith has changed little from medieval times: an ancient pattern of often tiny, irregular fields surrounded by Cornish hedges, isolated farmsteads and hamlets.

55. CARBIS BAY

The large sheltered beach of perfect white sand looks out on to St Ives Bay. Nestled between high wooded cliffs, Carbis Bay is on the St Ives branch line, one of the most scenic rail routes in the country.

56. ST IVES

The Island is a promontory which flanks Porthmeor Beach. It is seen here from the cemetery.

57. ST IVES

Voted one of the Best Seaside Towns in the UK, St Ives is home to the Tate St Ives, many superb restaurants and several stunning beaches. Its lichen-clad rooftops tumble down to the picturesque harbour.

58. GWITHIAN BEACH

With miles of golden sands stretching from Hayle Estuary to Godrevy Point, Gwithian Beach is big enough to accommodate everyone - families, walkers, horse riders and especially watersports lovers. From bodyboarding to kite surfing, the conditions looking out on to St Ives Bay are perfect.

60. PORTHTOWAN

The sandy beaches and dunes (towans) have ensured Porthtowan's popularity as a seaside resort since Victorian times. Very popular with surfers, Porthtowan hosts a number of surfing festivals throughout the year.

62. MAWGAN PORTH

A popular beach with fine yellow sand near Newquay is a favourite with surfers, bathers and sand-castle builders.

63. WATERGATE BAY

The stunning 2-mile expanse of sand and rolling Atlantic waves make Watergate Bay the perfect spot for all manner of watersports.

64. CORNISH HEDGE

As many motorists have found to their cost, the traditional Cornish Hedge is a stone-faced earth hedgebank with bushes or trees growing along the top and wild flowers and greenery tumbling down the sides. It is a haven for wildlife.

65. PORTHCOTHAN

A few miles south of Padstow lies the lovely sandy beach of Porthcothan. It is sheltered by sand dunes and craggy headlands, with fine golden sand and rock pools at low tide. There are excellent cliff walks to east and west.

66. PADSTOW

A busy working fishing port, Padstow is a very popular tourist destination. Situated on the west side of the Camel estuary, it is an area of outstanding natural beauty, sandy beaches and excellent sailing. Quaint, narrow streets lead down to the picture perfect harbour - the last sight of Cornwall for many a Cornishman and his family as they left for a new life in North America following the collapse of tin mining. Today it is home to a small fleet of day fishing boats. Padstow's 'Obby 'Oss festival heralds the arrival of summer. The two teams of the 'Old' and 'Blue Ribbon' 'osses parade around town from midnight on 1st May.

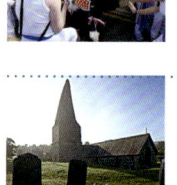

68. ST. ENODOC

The chapel-of-ease of St Enodoc is hidden away amongst the sand dunes. Surrounded by the fairways of St Enodoc Golf Course, the church was first built in 1430. Sir John Betjeman is buried here.

69. TEMPLE CHURCH

The church of St Catherine in the tiny hamlet of Temple on Bodmin Moor, is built on the former site of a Templar chapel. In the 16th century, the church became famous as the South West's own Gretna Green.

70. PORT ISAAC

The early 14th century fishing village of Port Isaac is one of the most attractive in Cornwall. Its narrow alleys and 'opes' and white-washed cottages wind down the steep hillsides to the sea. Today fishermen still work from the Platt, landing a daily catch of fish, crab and lobster.

72. PORT GAVERNE

Only a few yards up the coast from Port Isaac, Port Gaverne used to be the main port for shipping slate from Delabole Quarry. Now a small holiday hamlet, the sandy beach has an abundance of rock pools at low tide and is a favourite with children.

74. BOSCASTLE

Medieval Boscastle has a most distinctive natural S-shaped harbour created by the confluence of three rivers. It is protected by two stone walls which were built in 1584 by Sir Richard Grenville. The harbour is almost invisible from the sea and has played host to many a pirate, smuggler and wrecker over the years. The village itself has cottages dating back to the 15th century and snakes up the steep-sided Valency valley. In 2004 a devastating flash flood, caused when this normally gentle river burst its banks, resulted in extensive damage to low lying buildings with 115 cars swept into the harbour and 100 people rescued by helicopter. The final rebuilding work was completed in 2008.

76. BUDE

The seaside town of Bude lies on the Atlantic Heritage Coast and has been a favourite holiday resort since Victorian times. Fine sandy beaches are popular with families and the Atlantic rollers with surfers. The famous Bude canal is a testament to 19th century engineering and walks along its banks pass through some of the most unspoilt scenery in all of North Tamar.

78. GREAT FLAT LODE

The Great Flat Lode is an enormous, almost horizontal, ore-bearing lode situated just south of Carn Brea. Named for its relative flatness in relation to the ground and unusual in that most lodes run perpendicularly, it proved easier to work for the mines which sprang up along its length. The area has recently achieved 'World Heritage Status' and the 7 1/2 mile Great Flat Lode Trail encompasses all the major mines of the Camborne-Redruth area.

80. THE HURLERS

This Bronze Age stone temple lies near the moorland village of Minions and is built in a pass between the Rivers Fowey and Lynher, the sides of Stowe's Hill and Caradon rising to north and south. Such circles are often found at suitable meeting places for people and traders. There are three circles in total, consisting of 9, 14 and 15 stones each. Two of the circles were once linked by a granite pathway. All the stones have been carefully erected to appear the same height. The name The Hurlers, refers to a medieval legend whereby the circles are said to be men, turned to stone for playing the Celtic game of hurling on a Sunday.

82. CARN BREA CASTLE

The hilltop site of Carn Brea near Redruth has far reaching views and has had human settlements there since Neolithic times. The castle was originally medieval and is built within the ramparts of the Iron Age hillfort. It has been much restored and extended over the years.

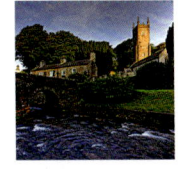

83. ALTARNUN

Altarnun, on the edge of Bodmin Moor nestles in the sheltered valley of Penpont Water. The village takes its name from the 6th century church of St Nonna whose fine Cornish cross still stands before the current 15th century church.

84. EDEN PROJECT

'The world's largest greenhouse', the Eden Project has become a world-famous tourist attraction and is at the forefront of educating and informing us about our natural world. The project is constructed in a disused clay pit near St Austell and consists of enormous biomes housing plants from the Humid Tropics regions of the world and the Warm Temperate regions as well as educational resources and extensive outdoor planting.

94. MISTY DAWN

Pre-dawn mist lies in the valleys of East Cornwall.

WRITERS

Writer	Page
Denys Val Baker	19
J M Barrie	20
Sven Berlin	11, 52
Beroul	26
Rodney Bewes	35
William Borlase	42
George Borrow	47, 82
William Camden	81
John le Carre	60
James F Cobb	79
George Alexander Cooke	19, 84
Derek Cooper	11
Arthur Quiller-Couch	16, 32
Margaret Ann Courtney	49
Frederick J Cowles	72
Dinah Craik	28, 36
Charles Dance	41
Arthur Conan Doyle	3
Gilbert and Sullivan	45
Thomas Hardy	75
John Harris	62
Robert Stephen Hawker	76
George Henwood	28
Barbara Hepworth	55
Henry Jenner	81
Francis Kilvert	36
Steve Knightley	82
John Leland	30, 56, 66
S P B Mais	15, 56, 59
Katherine Mansfield	15
Daphne du Maurier	20
Beunans Meriasek	25
Thomas Mills	45
Geoffrey of Monmouth	25, 69
H V Morton	30
Friedrich Max Muller	55
J L W Page	71
Rosamunde Pilcher	51
Rev Richard Polwhele	32
Henry Quick	12
Cyrus Redding	72
J K Rowling	64
George Bernard Shaw	71
Henry C Shelley	12
Paul Theroux	20, 59
E V Thompson	22
John Thomas	42
J C Trewin	35
C C Vyvyan	32
John Wesley	16
West Briton	26, 41, 79
Walter White	66
Colin Wilson	22
Virginia Woolf	51

89

MAP AND INDEX

Altarnun	83	Helford	32, 33	Port Isaac	65
Boscastle	74, 75	King Harry Ferry	25	Porthcothan	48, 49
Bude	76, 77	Kingsand	13	Porthcurno Beach	50
Cadgwith	35	Kynance	37	Porthgwarra Beach	41
Calstock	10	Landscape near	94	Porthleven	3, 60,
Carbis Beach	55	Fowey	19	Porthtowan	61
Carn Brea Castle	82	Lanteglos-by-Fowey	14, 15	Rinsey	40
Cawsand	12	Looe	26	Road sign	47
Charlestown Harbour	24	Malpas	62	Saltash	11
Chûn Quoit	45	Mawgan Porth	22, 23	Sennen	51
Coast Path	36	Mevagissey	46	St Enodoc	68
Combe	29	Mousehole	28	St Ives	56, 57
Cornish Hedge	64	Old Kea	66, 67	St Michael's Mount	42, 43
Coverack	34	Padstow	4	Temple Church	69
Eden Project	84, 85	Pednevounder Beach	18	The Hurlers	80, 81
Falmouth	30, 31	Pencarrow Head	54	Truro Cathedral	27
Fowey	21	Penwith	44	Watergate Beach	63
Great Flat Lode	78, 79	Penzance	16, 17	Wheal Prosper	40
Gunwalloe Church Cove	38	Polperro	20		
Gurnard's Head	52, 53	Polruan	72, 73		
Gwithian Beach	58, 59	Port Gaverne	70, 71		

76
77
75
74
70
71
72
73
66
68
67
64
65
69
63
83
62
80
81
10
3
84
85
61
60
59
54
56
24
58
57
21
19
94
52
55
27
14
15
20
18
53
22
17
16
26
45
82
28
29
23
11
25
78
79
12
51
44
13
47
42
43
30
49
31
50
48
4
40
41
32
33
38
34
37
35
36

PHOTOGRAPHER'S NOTES

In my earlier book, 'From Cornwall With Love', I included a page of tongue in cheek notes about photography with one more serious remark.

"Photography is like fishing. You go out in the morning with no idea of what the trip will bring. Sometimes luck is on your side and all your crab pots are full of prime Lobsters. Other times you get nothing." This paragraph has now been repeated and quoted by many photographers around the world on the world wide web. It is still my attitude towards photography. I can go out for a day and get very little that is usable and on another occasion get many good images.

'From Cornwall With Love' was at the forefront of a technical breakthrough. A small repro bureaux in Falmouth were one of the first in the world to provide full colour desktop publishing by producing litho film separations with the text included. Even the UK's biggest book printer took another couple of years to catch up. They were also one of the first to understand the value of archiving my digital scans. Since then there have been technical revolutions in photography with the coming of digital cameras and digital preparation for printing. What once needed hundreds of thousands of pounds of investment can now be done by my relatively modest computer sitting on my desk at home. What used to cost £5,000 to originate a colour book now costs nothing more than pressing a few keys on a computer and burning a CD. This brings advantages and disadvantages. On the plus side I am now in control of all stages of the image processing. The downside is that it entails much more work indoors. In view of the changes I make the following updated observations.

1/ Landscape photography has gone from being a healthy activity out of doors to an unhealthy activity tied to a computer.
2/ The internet has made a lot of things easier but in many ways it has merely shifted the effort. Instead of spending wasted hours sitting in my car waiting for the sun to shine I now spend wasted hours looking up the weather on the web.
3/ Instead of the nightmare of running out of film or scratching a slide I now have the headache of losing a file on my myriad hard drives.
4/ No matter what amazing light I captured on film there was always a 'know-it-all' who would dismiss the result with a scornful cry 'Filters!'. Now the put-down is 'Photoshop'.
5/ One of these days, to satisfy the nerds, I'll publish a book just showing the histograms.
6/ I have been criticised by some photographers for stating that photographs are not repeatable. They live in those boring countries where the sun shines exactly the same everyday for months on end. Cornwall is different from minute to minute, tide to tide, day to day and season to season. It might be frustrating being a photographer in Cornwall, but it is never dull.

With special thanks to Karen Forster for all the work on researching the text and permissions. Also thanks to everyone at Atmosphere for their invaluable help.

ACKNOWLEDGEMENTS

The quotation from Spring at Land's End by Denys Val Baker is reproduced with kind permission of Martin Val Baker

The quotations from Pride of the Peacock and The Coat of Many Colours by Sven Berlin are reproduced with kind permission of Mrs Julia Berlin

The quotation from A Likely Story the autobiography of Rodney Bewes, published by Century is reproduced with kind permission of The Random House Group Ltd

The quotation from Snail Eggs and Samphire by Derek Cooper is reproduced with kind permission of Pan Macmillan, London. Copyright Derek Cooper 2000

The quotation from the Diary of Charles Dance on the making of Ladies in Lavender is reproduced with permission of Charles Dance and Independent Talent Group Ltd

The quotation from Barbara Hepworth A Pictorial Autobiography is reproduced with permission of Tate Publishing

The quotation from The Shell Seekers by Rosamunde Pilcher is reproduced with permission of Hodder & Stoughton Limited

The quotation from Cousin Jack, written by Steve Knightley of Show of Hands is reproduced with kind permission of Show of Hands www.showofhands.co.uk

The quotations from The Kingdom by the Sea by Paul Theroux are reproduced with permission of The Wylie Agency (UK) Ltd., London on behalf of Copyright © Paul Theroux, 1983

The quotations from The Lost Years by E V Thompson are reproduced with permission of Little, Brown Book Group

The quotation from Up From The Lizard by J C Trewin is reproduced with kind permission of Ion Trewin on behalf of the estate of J C Trewin

The quotation by Colin Wilson from My Cornwall edited by Michael Williams, published by Bossiney Books is reproduced with kind permission of Colin Wilson

The quotation from A Cornish Year by C C Vyvyan is reproduced by kind permission of Elizabeth J Bourne

The quotation from In Search of England by H V Morton Copyright © Marion Wasdell and Brian de Villiers) is reproduced by permission of Methuen

The quotation from The Magic of Cornwall by Frederick I Cowles is reproduced with kind permission of Michael W Cowles

The quotation from Daphne du Maurier's diary quoted in Daphne by Judith Cook, published by Corgi is reproduced with kind permission of Curtis Brown Group Ltd, London on behalf of the Estate of Daphne du Maurier. Copyright © Daphne du Maurier 1991

The quotation from The Doctor's Dilemma by George Bernard Shaw is reproduced with kind permission of The Society of Authors, on behalf of the Bernard Shaw Estate

The quotation from The Little Drummer Girl by John le Carre © David Cornwell 1983 is reproduced with permission of Curtis Brown Group Ltd

The quotation from Moments of Being by Virginia Woolf published by Hogarth Press is reproduced with permission of the executors of the Virginia Woolf Estate and The Random House Group Limiited

The quotation from Harry Potter and the Deathly Hallows by J K Rowling is reproduced with permission of The Christopher Little Literary Agency

Every effort has been made to contact all copyright holders. Should the publishers have made any mistakes in attribution, we will be pleased to make the necessary arrangements at the first opportunity.

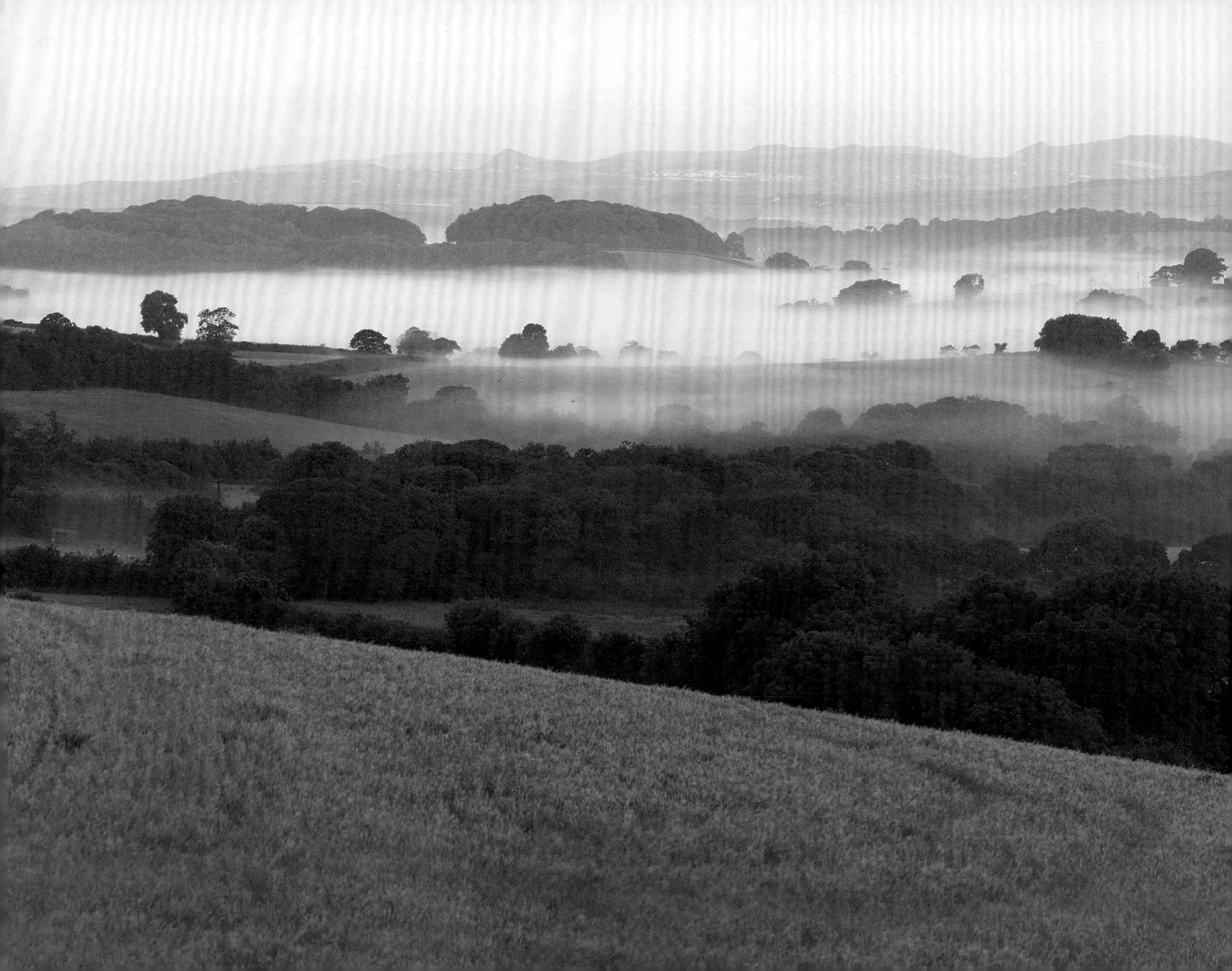